RUSSIA

A PRIMARY SOURCE CULTURAL GUIDE

Suzanne J. Murdico

The Rosen Publishing Group's
PowerPlus Books™
New York

For Vinnie

Published in 2005 by The Rosen Publishing Group, Inc.
29 East 21st Street, New York, NY 10010

First Edition

Library of Congress Cataloging-in-Publication Data

Murdico, Suzanne J.
Russia: a primary source cultural guide/by Suzanne J. Murdico.
p. cm.—(Primary sources of world cultures)
Includes bibliographical references and index.
ISBN 1-4042-2913-2 (library binding)
1. Russia (Federation)—Juvenile literature.
I. Title. II. Series.
DK510.23.M87 2004
947—dc22

2004000754

Manufactured in the United States of America

Cover images: Background: Manuscript for *The Queen of Spades* by Peter Tchaikovsky. Left: St. Basil's Cathedral in Red Square, Moscow. Right: A performer in ethnic dress on May Day in Red Square.

Photo credits: cover (background), p. 78 © Roger-Viollet, Paris/Bridgeman Art Library; cover (middle), pp. 5 (middle), 7, 56, 94 © Scott S.Warren/Aurora Photos; cover (bottom), p. 111 (bottom) © Adam Tanner/The Image Works; pp. 3, 118, 120 © 2002 GeoAtlas; pp. 4 (top), 15, 110 © Hans-Jürgen Burkard/Aurora Photos; pp. 4 (middle), 33 (bottom) © Maria Stenzel/National Geographic Image Collection; pp. 4 (bottom), 35 © Peter Turnley/Corbis; pp. 5 (top), 51 © 2000 Novosti/Topham/The Image Works; pp. 5 (bottom), 86 © UPPA/Topham/The Image Works; pp. 6, 52 © Cary Wolinsky/IPN/Aurora Photos; p. 8 © Wolfgang Kaehler/Corbis; p. 9 © Maggie Steber/Aurora Photos; p. 10 © Jim Brandenburg/Minden Pictures; pp. 11, 55 (top) © Davide Monteleone/Contrasto/Redux; pp. 12, 34 © AFP/Getty Images; pp. 13 (top), 65, 106 (top) © Thomas Dworzak/Magnum Photos; pp. 13 (bottom), 50, 92 © Abbas/Magnum Photos; p. 14 © Nigel Marven/Naturepl.com; pp. 16, 17 (top) © Konrad Wothe/Minden Pictures; p. 17 (bottom) © Michio Hoshino/Minden Pictures; pp. 18, 40, 44, 61, 69, 79, 82 (top) © akg-images; pp. 19, 20 (top) © The Art Archive/Hermitage Museum Saint Petersburg/Dagli Orti (A); p. 20 (bottom) © Novosti/Bridgeman Art Library; p. 21 © Slavic and Baltic Division, The New York Public Library, Astor, Lenox and Tilden Foundations; pp. 22, 45 © Tretyakov Gallery, Moscow, Russia/Bridgeman Art Library; p. 23 (top) © Erich Lessing/Art Resource, NY; p. 23 (bottom) © Corbis; pp. 24, 29, 49, 71, 84 © Topham/The Image Works; p. 26 © Kreuels/Bilderberg/Aurora Photos; p. 27 © Hulton/Archive/Getty Images; p. 28 © The Art Archive/Dagli Orti; p. 30 (top) © Henri Cartier-Bresson/Magnum Photos; p. 30 (bottom), 59 © Bruno Barbey/Magnum Photos; pp. 31, 76 (top) © Roberto Koch/Contrasto/Redux; p. 32 © Reuters/Corbis; p. 33 (top) © Antonio Scattolon/A3/Contrasto/Redux; p. 37 (top) © The State Russian Museum/Corbis; pp. 38, 100 (bottom), 119 © AP/Wide World Photos; p. 39 (top) © Roberto Koch/Contrasto/Redux; p. 39 (bottom) © Jonathan Smith/Lonely Planet Images; p. 41 © Mary Evans Picture Library; p. 42 © Archives Charmet/Bridgeman Art Library; pp. 46, 81 (top) © Bettmann/Corbis; pp. 47, 81 (bottom) © Photofest; pp. 48, 55 (bottom) © Hideo Haga/HAGA/The Image Works; p. 53 © Nicolas Tikhomiroff/Magnum Photos; p. 54 © Elliott Erwitt/Magnum Photos; p. 57 © Joanna B. Pinneo/Aurora Photos; p. 58 © Archivo Iconografico, S.A./Corbis; p. 60 © Mauro Galligani/Contrasto/Redux; p. 62 © Jeff Greenberg/The Image Works; pp. 63, 93 (bottom) © Josef Polleross/The Image Works; p. 64 © Museum of the Holy Ma'sumeh Shrine, Qom, Iran/Bridgeman Art Library; p. 66 © Gueorgui Pinkhassov/Magnum Photos; pp. 67, 107 © Sean Sprague/The Image Works; p. 68 © ARS, NY/Scala/Art Resource, NY; p. 70 (top) © Alinari Archives/Corbis; p. 70 (bottom) © Daniel Frasnay/akg-images; p. 72 (top) © Museum of the Revolution, Moscow, Russia/Giraudon/Bridgeman Art Library; p. 72 (bottom) © Comstock Images/Matton Images; p. 73 © Scala/Art Resource, NY; p. 74 © Benoit Roland/The Image Works; p. 75 © Steve Vidler/SuperStock; p. 76 (bottom) © Bill Bachmann/The Image Works; pp. 77, 97 (bottom) © Chris Anderson/Aurora Photos; 82 (bottom) © Sovfoto/Eastfoto; pp. 83, 98 © Novosti/Topham/The Image Works; p. 85 © Georgi G. Shablovsky/Lonely Planet Images; p. 87 (top) © Ferdinando Scianna/Magnum Photos; p. 87 (bottom) © Pete Oxford/Naturepl.com; p. 88 © Hans-Jürgen Burkard/Bilderberg/Aurora Photos; p. 89 © Seitre/Peter Arnold, Inc; p. 90 © Novosti/Sovfoto; p. 91 © Eising FoodPhotography/StockFood; p. 93 (top) © Jörg Heimann/Bilderberg/Peter Arnold, Inc; p. 95 © Steve Raymer/Corbis; p. 96 © Marc Garanger/Corbis; p. 97 (top) © Clark James Mishler/IPN/Aurora Photos; p. 100 (top) © Jay LaPrete/Icon SMI; p. 101 © Lynn Johnson/Aurora Photos; p. 102 © David Turnley/Corbis; p. 103 © Charles Steiner/The Image Works; p. 104 © Snark/Art Resource, NY; p. 106 (bottom) © Paul Almasy/Corbis; p. 108 © Hans-Jürgen Burkard/Bilderberg/Peter Arnold, Inc; p. 109 © Peter Essick/Aurora Photos; p. 111 (top) © Eligio Paoni/Contrasto/Redux; p. 121 © Patrick Johns/Corbis.

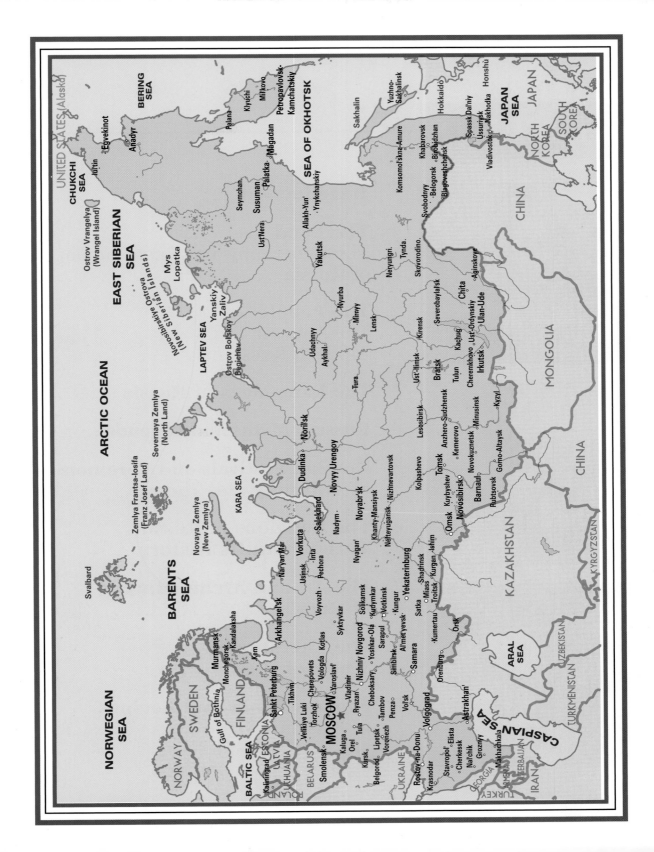

CONTENTS

INTRODUCTION

I cannot forecast to you the action of Russia.
It is a riddle wrapped in a mystery inside an enigma.

—Winston Churchill (1874–1965)

The largest country in the world, Russia covers an area of approximately 6.6 million square miles (17 million square kilometers). That's nearly twice the size of Canada, which is the world's second-largest country. Russia is so vast that it extends halfway around the Northern Hemisphere, spanning two continents—Europe and Asia—and eleven time zones. A train trip on the Trans-Siberian Railway from Moscow in the west to Vladivostok in the east takes seven days. At Russia's northeastern tip, only 49 miles (78 kilometers) across the Bering Strait separate Russia from Alaska in the United States.

Russia is a land of striking contrasts. Wide, flat plains in the south meet high, snow-covered mountain peaks in the north. Temperatures range from extremely cold in winter to very hot in summer.

In terms of population, Russia ranks sixth in the world, behind China, India, the United States, Indonesia, and Brazil. The majority of Russia's people are ethnic Russians, meaning that their ancestors were an early Slavic people called the Russians. In addition to ethnic Russians, about 100 minority ethnic groups live in Russia today. Although the majority of people in Russia speak Russian, many ethnic groups also speak their own language. Russian Orthodoxy is the main religion in Russia, but several other religions are also practiced.

At left is St. Basil's Cathedral, located in Moscow's Red Square. St. Basil's Cathedral has nine chapels, each with its own decorative, onion-shaped dome. Today, St. Basil's is a museum and no longer a place of worship. Above: Despite its cold climate, the Siberian countryside is home to many mammalian species such as reindeer, moose, and bears.

It's hard to believe that this peaceful lake was once an active volcano, bubbling with lava. In Kamchatka, many volcanoes are still active. The Kamchatka volcanoes are constantly being studied by volcanologists from around the world.

Russia is a very old country with a rich and varied history involving several invasions and revolutions. This history, which dates back to AD 800, began with a European state founded by the East Slavs. In the thirteenth century, Mongol hordes invaded the country. Over time, Russia gained a great deal of territory, and many different groups of people came to live in the country.

For about 500 years, czars ruled the Russian Empire. The czars lived in luxury and ruled with absolute power over the Russian people, most of whom were poor, uneducated peasants. Under the czars' rule, Russia did not keep pace with the industrial advancements taking place in western Europe in the 1700s and 1800s. The country's economy suffered.

During the late 1800s and early 1900s, the Russian people began to oppose the total control exercised by the czars. In 1917, Russian revolutionaries overthrew the government and removed the czar from power. The new Communist leaders who

A passenger on the Trans-Siberian Railway looks out on the Russian countryside near Irkutsk. The Trans-Siberian has three lines: Trans-Siberian, Trans-Manchurian, and Trans-Mongolian. The railways connect Moscow with Vladivostok, Ulaan Baatar, Mongolia, and Beijing, China.

took over believed that the government should own all of the country's land, businesses, and banks.

Under Communist rule, Russia reclaimed fourteen republics that had once been part of the Russian Empire. Together, Russia and these republics became the Union of Soviet Socialist Republics (USSR), or simply the Soviet Union. Although Soviet rule helped the country become industrialized, the people had few freedoms and no voice in government.

In 1991, a monumental event—a major turning point in twentieth-century history—occurred. The Soviet Union collapsed and Communist rule ended. Russia and the other republics of the Soviet Union split apart to form independent countries. Today, Russia is a democracy, where the people have more freedoms and can elect their own government representatives.

THE LAND

The Geography and Environment of Russia

Russia's landscape is generally divided into five main land regions. From west to east, they are the European Plain, the Ural Mountains, the West Siberian Plain, the Central Siberian Plateau, and the East Siberian Uplands. To the north of Russia lie the seas of the vast and very cold Arctic Ocean. Russia's neighbors to the west include Finland, Estonia, Latvia, Belarus, and Ukraine. On the west, Russia also borders the Baltic Sea and the Black Sea. To the south, Russia's neighbors include Georgia, Azerbaijan, Kazakhstan, Mongolia, China, and North Korea, along with the Caspian Sea. Russia's eastern edge is all coastline, bordering the Bering Sea, the Sea of Okhotsk, and the Sea of Japan, all of which flow into the Pacific Ocean.

The Ural Mountains, which run north to south, divide the continents of Europe and Asia. The Urals also divide Russia into western and eastern regions. Western Russian is generally known as European Russia, and eastern Russia is called Asian Russia.

European Russia

The majority of people in Russia live in European Russia, which includes the country's two largest cities: Moscow and St. Petersburg. Moscow, the capital city, is the

At left is the Dnieper River, which runs from Russia through Belarus and Ukraine. Ultimately the Dnieper flows into the Black Sea. The river is approximately 1,368 miles (2,200 km) in length. Above, passengers walk through Moscow's Kievskaya Station. Moscow's metro is the busiest subway system in the world. On an average day, about 9 million people use it.

On a winter day in Moscow, the Moskva River freezes over in the subzero degree weather. The Moskva River is a main source of water for the city of Moscow. The Moskva also flows through the cities of Voskresensk, Kolomna, and Mozhaysk.

Russian center of government, industry, transportation, and communications. With a population of nearly 8.4 million, Moscow is not only the largest city in Russia, but also one of the largest cities in the world. The Moskva River, or Moscow River, after which Moscow was named, flows through the city. St. Petersburg, the second-largest city in Russia, has a population of more than 4.6 million. It was built in 1703 and named after its founder, Peter the Great. Home of the world-famous Hermitage Museum, St. Petersburg is generally considered the cultural capital of Russia.

Much of the land in European Russia is flat, open plains, well suited for agriculture. The southern border of European Russia is marked by the Caucasus Mountains. At 18,510 feet (5,642 meters), Mount Elbrus in the Caucasus Mountains is the highest peak in Europe as well as in all of Russia. The Volga River, which flows throughout European Russia, is the longest river in Europe. Other important rivers in European Russia include the Don, Dnieper, Dvina, Pechora, and Neva. These rivers

Russian peasants lead a pack mule up a road in the Caucasus Mountains. The Caucasus Mountains create a natural border between Europe and Asia.

provide essential transportation routes. In addition to its many rivers, European Russia also borders on the largest lake in the world—the saltwater Caspian Sea.

Not many people live in the extreme northern region of European Russia, where the land is very cold and bleak and where very little vegetation grows. One exception is the city of Murmansk on the Kola Peninsula. An important Russian seaport and major center of the fishing industry, Murmansk is located on the Barents Sea. Although Murmansk lies within the Arctic Circle, the seaport is warmed by the Gulf Stream and stays free of ice.

Asian Russia

Just to the east of the Ural Mountains lies Asian Russia, which extends across the entire continent of Asia. The enormous landmass in this region often is simply referred to as Siberia. The long, extremely cold winters in Asian Russia

In early fall, the Siberian countryside is covered with vegetation. In parts of Siberia, the warmer months are humid and provide excellent conditions for coniferous trees and plants.

A blue sulphuric lake in a volcano crater in Kamchatka. Kamchatka is a peninsula the size of Japan. It is full of volcanoes and diverse wildlife. The region has one of the largest salmon populations in the world.

make most of this area less habitable than European Russia. The largest city in Siberia is Novosibirsk, with a population of 1.4 million. Omsk, Irkutsk, and Vladivostok are other important cities in Asian Russia. Much of Russia's rich mineral resources are located in central and eastern Siberia.

Some of Russia's most breathtaking scenery can be found in Asian Russia. In eastern Siberia, the vast Kamchatka Peninsula is home to about 25 active volcanoes and more than 100 dormant ones. Lake Baikal, located in south-central Siberia, is the largest freshwater lake in the world. Nicknamed the Blue Eye of Siberia, Lake Baikal is also the world's deepest lake, with a depth of 5,315 feet (1,620 m).

Soil and Vegetation

The land of Russia can be classified into four distinct zones. Each of these zones, which run in belts from east to west, has its own unique soil, vegetation, and wildlife. From north to south, they are the tundra, taiga, forest, and steppe.

The Land: The Geography and Environment of Russia

The zone in the northernmost part of Russia is the tundra. There, about half of the area has permanently frozen soil, or permafrost. Not many people live there because the long, harsh winters and brief summers make the region largely uninhabitable. Vegetation in the tundra is sparse, consisting mainly of hardy shrubs, small trees, grass, moss, and lichen. Animals living there include reindeer, polar bears, arctic foxes, snowy owls, and lemmings. Walruses and seals live in the icy waters of the northern seas, where they dine on the abundant supply of fish.

Just south of the tundra lies the taiga. This area is filled with evergreen trees, including fir, pine, cedar, and spruce. Some of the soil is marshy, and most is not suited for farming. Larger animals in this area include brown bears, elk, foxes, lynx, sables, and deer. Smaller animals in the taiga include squirrels, muskrats, and beavers.

The forest zone is located just below the taiga. In this area grows a wider variety of trees, such as birch, aspen, oak, maple, and elm. In some parts of the forest, the climate is fairly mild and the soil is suitable for agriculture. This area is home to antelope, foxes, and wolves.

Russia's southernmost zone, filled with flat plains, is called the steppe. In the northern steppe region, the land consists of wooded plains and meadows. The southern steppe region is mostly a prairie with no trees. Because the most fertile soil in Russia is found in the steppe, this zone is mainly farmland. The area's moderate temperatures and longer growing season also contribute to its suitability for agriculture. Small animals, including squirrels, mice, and mole rats, roam the steppe. The area's bird population includes geese, egrets, and cormorants.

A fisherman examines a freshly caught sturgeon on the banks of the Volga River. The Volga River Delta provides some of the best fishing in Europe and Asia.

Lake Baikal is not only one of the largest lakes in the world but also one of the oldest. Geologists believe the lake is between 25 and 30 million years old.

Climate

Russia's extreme northern location just below the Arctic Circle ensures that much of the country's climate is very cold for most of the year. The large mountain ranges to the east and south prevent the warming influences of the Pacific and Indian Oceans from reaching the country's interior. At the same time, the lack of mountains on the northern and western sides allows the cold influences from the Arctic and Atlantic Oceans to affect the climate.

Because spring and autumn are so short, Russia essentially has just two seasons—winter and summer. Russian winters typically last for at least six months in European Russia and for as long as ten months in parts of Siberia. Winter brings extremely cold temperatures, along with plenty of snow and freezing winds. Throughout the entire season, much of Russia remains snow covered, and many rivers and lakes stay frozen. In northeastern Siberia, winter temperatures can drop to an incredible low of -96° Fahrenheit (-71° Celsius). The average summer temperature in the same region is about 60°F (16°C) but can reach close to 100°F (38°C). Almost nowhere else in the world can there be found such an extreme range of temperatures.

Wildlife

Two of the animals in Russia merit special mention—the brown bear and the Siberian tiger. The brown bear, often referred to as the Russian brown bear, is the unofficial symbol of Russia. Adult brown bears are very large, typically weighing

A Russian grizzly takes a nap. Contrary to popular belief, grizzly is actually just another name for a brown bear.

between 300 and 550 pounds (136 and 227 kilograms). The Siberian brown bear is unusually large, weighing as much as 795 pounds (361 kg). Despite their size, brown bears are very fast, capable of running at speeds of up to 30 miles per hour (48 km/h). They are also strong swimmers. Brown bears eat fish and small animals, along with plants, berries, and honey. Although extinct in much of western Europe, brown bears still roam the forests of Russia.

Tigers are the largest of the big cats, and the Siberian tiger is the largest subspecies of tiger, weighing up to 660 pounds (299 kg). Siberian tigers hunt mainly elk and wild boars. Their back legs are longer than their front legs, allowing them to more easily jump on their prey. These longer back legs also make it easier for them to run through deep snow. Siberian tigers are an endangered species, with only an estimated 400 surviving in the wild. The majority of these tigers live in the birch forests of eastern Russia. The main threats to Siberian tigers are habitat destruction and poaching, or illegal hunting.

On the brink of extinction, Siberian tigers are a rare sight. The last population of Siberian tigers lives in Russia along the Sikhote-Alin mountain range.

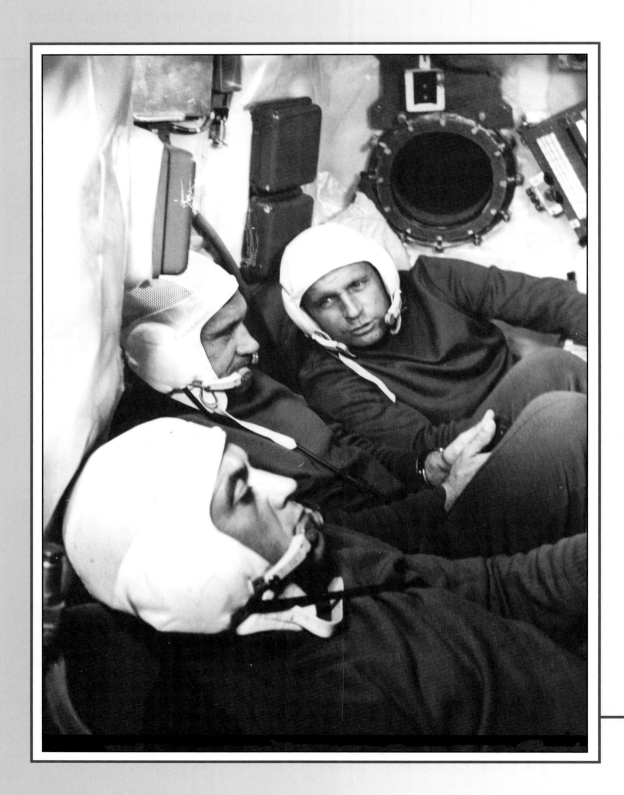

THE PEOPLE

2

The Ancient and Modern Russians

Early settlers in Russia were Slavic people who had traveled from central Asia to European Russia in the sixth century AD. Today's Russians, Ukrainians, and Belarusians are descendants of these early Slavs. For several hundred years, the Slavs worked as farmers, craftspeople, and traders. They built towns along the river trade routes of northern and western Russia and did well by trading with Scandinavia and eastern Europe. Because the Slavic towns were not united, however, they were invaded many times over the years.

Kievan Rus: Early Slavs

In the ninth century, a Viking tribe gained control of the Slavic lands. The Vikings brought the Slavs together and founded a new state called Kievan Rus. Kiev (in modern-day Ukraine) became the capital and most important city in Kievan Rus. Prince Vladimir, the ruler of Kiev, converted to Christianity in 988. After he made Christianity the state religion, most people under his rule also converted. They followed the faith of the Byzantine Empire, which was the Eastern Orthodox

At left, Russian cosmonauts Vladislav Volkov, Anatoly Filipchenko, and Viktor Gorbatko train in secret before their voyage on the *Soyuz 7* in 1969. Above is a fourth-century BC gold necklace excavated from Tolstaja Mogila Kurgan in Dnepropetrovsk. The necklace depicts ancient Scythians milking sheep and making clothes out of animal skins.

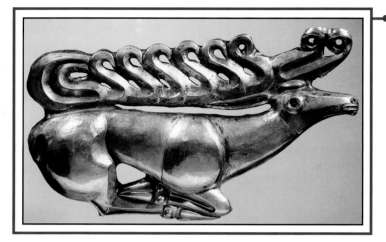

This gold stag was once a decoration on an ancient shield used by the Scythians. It was made during the seventh century BC.

Church. At that time, most Europeans were Roman Catholics. This difference in religion separated the people of Russia from the rest of Europe. On the other hand, it also helped them create their own unique culture.

Mongol Invasion

Kiev was a powerful city until the middle of the eleventh century. By then, other principalities of Kievan Rus had also become powerful. With no central government, however, many civil wars erupted. By the thirteenth century, these wars had weakened the power of Kievan Rus.

In 1237, a Mongol leader named Batu Khan led enormous armies of Mongols into Russia. Batu was a grandson of Genghis Khan, a legendary Mongol conqueror. These Mongols, known as Tatars, invaded Russia from central Asia. During the Mongol invasion, many

A page from a sixteenth-century medieval chronicle details the siege of Kozelsk in 1238. Batu Khan is pictured atop a horse, leading his men into battle.

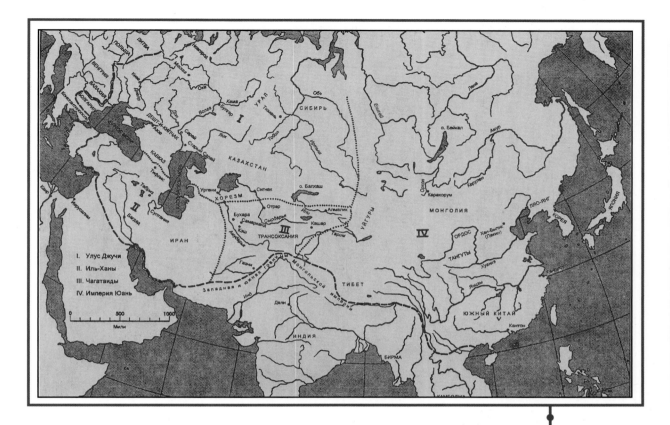

This map shows the Mongol-controlled land known as the Golden Horde during the late thirteenth century. Russia was conquered by Batu Khan. The area was called the Golden Horde because the Mongol armies camped in yellow tents.

Russian towns were destroyed. When the Mongol armies finally destroyed Kiev in 1240, Kievan Rus fell. Russia was then integrated into the Mongol Empire in a section known as the Golden Horde. The Mongols continued their occupation of Russia for nearly 250 years. Mongol rule finally came to an end in 1480, when Prince Ivan III (thereafter known as Ivan the Great) ousted the invaders. Ivan declared himself Russia's czar, which is Russian for "Caesar."

Reign of the Czars

Beginning with Ivan III, Russia's leaders became known as czars. In the mid-sixteenth century, Ivan IV became the first Russian ruler to be crowned czar. His reign was one of cruelty and terror, earning him the name Ivan the Terrible. Through his many land conquests, Russia's territory was greatly expanded. After Ivan's death, the Romanov family ruled Russia for the next 300 years.

A full-length portrait of Ivan the Terrible by Victor Mikhailovich Vasnetsov, painted in 1897. Ivan IV was crowned czar at the age of sixteen in 1547.

The Romanov Dynasty

The Romanov dynasty began with the reign of Michael Romanov in 1613 and ended in 1917 with Nicholas II and the Russian Revolution. The Romanov dynasty had a lasting influence, both positive and negative, on the people of Russia.

Peter the Great, a Romanov czar, encouraged greater contact with western Europe. During Peter's reign, Russian art, architecture, and engineering were influenced and modernized by European ideas. Peter gained more land for Russia, founded the city of St. Petersburg, and modernized the military. Under his rule, Russia became an important European power. Catherine the Great, a Romanov empress, supported the arts and sciences and promoted European culture in Russia. Under her rule, the Russian Empire expanded greatly.

An anonymous portrait of Empress Catherine the Great of Russia. Catherine enjoyed writing, and during her reign she wrote plays, stories, and memoirs.

Serfs

While the czars lived in great luxury, most Russian people lived as serfs. Serfs were peasants who lived and worked on land that was owned by a wealthy landlord. Serfs were forced to pay high rents, usually in the form of work done for the landlord in addition to a share of the serf's own harvest. In many ways, serfs were hardly better off than slaves. They owned no land, had few civil rights, and generally lived in poverty. Serfdom in Russia was eventually abolished in 1856.

The Bolsheviks

In 1894, Nicholas II became Russia's last czar. By that time, the Russian people had become more and more discontented with the rule of the czars. With increased industrialization, unhappy workers began to protest. They were drawn to several

This 1861 drawing depicts Russian serfs in a small village. Under Catherine the Great, nobles were given complete control over serfs and their land.

political movements that promised social reform in Russia. One of these political groups was called the Russian Social Democratic Labor Party, which later divided into the Bolsheviks (members of the majority) and the Mensheviks (members of the minority). The leader of the Bolsheviks was V. I. (Vladimir Ilyich) Lenin.

On January 22, 1905, thousands of Russian workers marched peacefully to the Winter Palace in St. Petersburg. There, they were going to request reforms from Czar Nicholas II. Although the marchers were not armed, government soldiers opened fired on them. Hundreds of people were injured or killed, and the day became known as Bloody Sunday.

When World War I began in 1914, Russia, France, and Great Britain joined forces to fight against Austria-Hungary and Germany. They later became known as the Allies. During the war, the Russian people suffered. Many Russian soldiers fighting on the front lines had not been trained and were killed in battle. On the home front, the Russian people had severe food and fuel shortages because so much money and supplies were needed for the war effort.

The Romanov Czars

1613–1645	Michael Romanov
1645–1676	Alexis I
1676–1682	Fyodor III
1682–1689	Ivan V
1682–1725	Peter I, or Peter the Great
1725–1727	Catherine I
1727–1730	Peter II
1730–1740	Anna
1740–1741	Ivan VI
1741–1762	Elizabeth
1762–1762	Peter III
1762–1796	Catherine II, or Catherine the Great
1796–1801	Paul I
1801–1825	Alexander I
1825–1855	Nicholas I
1855–1881	Alexander II
1881–1894	Alexander III
1894–1917	Nicholas II

1917 Russian Revolution

Two major Russian revolutions occurred in 1917—the February Revolution and the October Revolution. In March 1917 (February by the old Russian calendar),

At left is a photograph taken at the Winter Palace on Bloody Sunday, January 22, 1905. After the massacre, workers were even more convinced that Nicholas II was a cruel, unsympathetic ruler. In response to Bloody Sunday, there was a general protest.

A panorama of the sparkling city of St. Petersburg from the Neva River. A network of palace-lined rivers runs through the city. St. Petersburg is often nicknamed the Venice of the North.

the Russian people rioted over the food and fuel shortages. The riots took place in the Russian capital of Petrograd (now St. Petersburg). Government soldiers were sent to stop the riots, but instead, they joined them. By that time, Czar Nicholas II had lost all of his political power and support. A temporary government was set up, and Nicholas was forced to step down from the throne. He and his family were taken as prisoners.

By autumn of 1917, the Russian people were tired and hungry and most didn't want to face another long, bitter winter at war. Seizing this opportunity, Bolshevik leader Lenin planned the October Revolution. On November 7, 1917 (October 25 by the old Russian calendar), Bolshevik-led armies began their revolt. They soon took control of Petrograd and the Winter Palace, which had become the headquarters for the temporary government. The Bolsheviks overthrew the temporary government and created a new government led by Lenin.

The new Bolshevik government negotiated a cease-fire to withdraw from World War I. In the process, however, Russia lost a great deal of its territory. The Bolshevik government also moved Russia's capital to Moscow. In July 1918, Bolshevik revolutionaries executed Czar Nicholas II and his family, permanently ending Russia's reign of the czars. The Bolsheviks changed the name of their party from the Russian Social Democratic Labor Party to the Russian Communist Party.

Life Under Communist Rule

Between 1918 and 1920, the country was engaged in a bitter civil war. Communist forces, known as the Red Army, battled against anti-Communist forces, known as the White Army, for control of Russia. Eventually, the Communists gained control. Many Russians were unhappy with the new Communist government and protested against its policies. In 1921, Lenin introduced a new policy in which much of Russia's economy, including transportation, banking, and trade, came under government control. By the end of 1922, Russia had joined with three other territories to form a new country called the Union of Soviet Socialist Republics (USSR), or the Soviet Union. These were the first of the country's union republics. Over the next eighteen years, more union republics would join the USSR, bringing the total number to fifteen by 1940.

Lenin died in 1924. After a fierce power struggle by several leading members of the Communist Party, Joseph Stalin took over as leader of the party and the Soviet Union. Stalin's new economic policies focused on creating large, government-run farms by combining smaller farms that had been privately owned. The policies also stressed the development of heavy industry. Stalin's policies were not well received by many Soviet citizens. To quell the opposition, Stalin had his secret police arrest millions of Russian people. Many were sent to prison labor camps in Siberia. Others were executed. In this way, Stalin removed any potential threats to his dictatorship of the Soviet Union.

Life under Communist rule was very difficult for the Soviet people. The government placed severe

This photograph of Joseph Stalin was taken in 1935. "Stalin" was a nickname that the leader eventually adopted. In Russian, the name means "steel."

Leaders of the Soviet Union	
1917–1924	Vladimir Ilyich Lenin
1924–1953	Joseph Stalin
1953–1964	Nikita Khrushchev
1964–1982	Leonid Brezhnev
1982–1984	Yuri Andropov
1984–1985	Konstantin Chernenko
1985–1991	Mikhail Gorbachev

Leaders of the Russian Federation

1991–1999	Boris Yeltsin
2000–present	Vladimir Putin

restrictions on the country's citizens, taking away many of their freedoms. Writers and artists were no longer allowed freedom of expression. The Communist Party forced them to work in a style called Socialist Realism. In this manner, all literature and artwork was supposed to glorify Communism, create positive role models, and show happy Soviet workers. Because the Communist Party deemed religion to be unnecessary, people were discouraged from religious worship. Soviet students were instructed that God didn't exist.

The USSR in World War II

During the 1930s, Adolf Hitler rose to power in Germany. One of the German dictator's main goals was to invade and conquer Europe. In 1939, Germany and the USSR became allies when they signed a nonaggression pact. The pact stated that neither country would attack the other country. In September 1939, World War II began with Germany's invasion of Poland. While German troops invaded Poland from the west, Soviet troops approached and occupied the eastern third of the country.

The German-Soviet alliance quickly dissolved, however, when Germany invaded the Soviet Union in June 1941. Although it first appeared as though

БЕССМЕРТНЫЙ ВОЖДЬ ОКТЯБРЯ
ЛЕНИН
УКАЗАЛ НАМ ПУТЬ К
ПОБЕДЕ
ДА ЗДРАВСТВУЕТ
ЛЕНИНИЗМ
К 7-ГОДОВЩИНЕ ОКТЯБРЬСКОЙ ПОБЕДЫ.

A poster from 1925 commemorates seven years of Leninism in Russia. The poster reads, "The immortal October leader Lenin has shown us the way to victory; long live Leninism!"

A photograph taken in 1935 shows the Red Army practicing dangerous tank maneuvers. The Red Army wanted to test the durability of its new tanks.

Germany might succeed in its invasion, the German troops were not prepared for the bitterly cold Soviet winters. Their clothing wasn't warm enough to withstand the subzero Fahrenheit temperatures, and many suffered from frostbite. Thousands of German soldiers froze to death. For the Soviet Union, the turning point in World War II was the Battle of Stalingrad (now Volgograd) in 1943. During that battle, the Soviet armies defeated the German troops and drove them out of the country. The Soviet forces helped put an end to the war when they captured Berlin—Germany's capital—on May 2, 1945.

The Cold War

Although the Soviet Union had cooperated with the United States during World War II, the alliance didn't last for long. Relations between the two countries had been strained since 1917, when the Communist government came into being. After World War II, the tension increased. The Soviet Union extended its Communist control into Eastern Europe and placed restrictions on travel, trade, and communication between the East and the West. The United States didn't approve of Communism and wanted all countries to be independent democracies. Mutual distrust between Communist and non-Communist countries developed into a long, intense struggle and rivalry that became known as the Cold War.

At times, the Cold War became so heated that it threatened to erupt into World War III. That never happened, however. After the death of Joseph Stalin in

Women and children line up in front of a grocery store. During the time of Stalin, provisions were scarce and lines for goods were often long.

1953, Nikita Khrushchev took over as leader of the Soviet Union. He eased some of the restrictions that had been put into effect during the Stalin era. He also helped to improve relations between the Soviet Union and the West. In 1964, Khrushchev was overthrown, and Leonid Brezhnev took control of the USSR. During his rule, Brezhnev tried to further improve U.S.-Soviet relations. But several key issues, including the 1979 Soviet invasion of Afghanistan, only served to increase tensions between East and West.

Collapse of the Soviet Union

By the end of the 1970s, people in the Soviet-controlled countries of Eastern Europe were becoming more and

In Odessa, crowds examine posters that call for *glasnost* (openness). Under Mikhail Gorbachev's leadership, there was a greater ability to have political discussions and to consider reform in the society.

A photograph of Mikhail Gorbachev taken in 1991. Gorbachev tried to institute reforms in the Soviet Union and is admired in the United States for ending the Cold War.

more discontented with Communism. In 1985, major changes began to take place in the Soviet Union with the rise of a new leader—Mikhail Gorbachev. When he took over, the country was confronted with serious economic problems. Enormous military expenses had caused many of these problems. In addition, the use of outdated technology and equipment in industry slowed production. This inefficient system created many shortages of food, consumer goods, and housing and led to long shopping lines and crowded living conditions for Soviet citizens.

Gorbachev's Reforms

In an effort to improve the situation in the Soviet Union, Gorbachev launched a policy of economic restructuring known as *perestroika* (restructuring). With this plan, the new Soviet leader tried to reform the country's economy by decreasing the amount of control that the government had over it. Gorbachev's goal was to stimulate economic growth and improve the efficiency of Soviet industry. Ultimately, though, perestroika failed. One policy introduced by Gorbachev and approved by the Soviet people was known as glasnost, or "openness." With this policy, Soviet citizens were granted greater freedom of expression in literature, art, and politics.

By the end of the 1980s, people in many Soviet republics were demanding more freedom from the central government. There was also increased nationalistic and ethnic infighting. In 1990, the Russian Republic declared limited independence from the Soviet Union under Boris Yeltsin. In July 1991, Gorbachev agreed to sign a treaty that would reorganize the Soviet Union and provide some other republics with more independence. However, just before the treaty was to be signed, conservative Communist Party leaders tried to overthrow Gorbachev's government. Yeltsin supported Gorbachev and rallied the people against the coup. The coup was unsuccessful, but it was the beginning of the end for Gorbachev's leadership.

Boris Yeltsin waves to a crowd of demonstrators protesting the overthrow of Soviet president Mikhail Gorbachev in the summer of 1991. The failure of the coup ultimately lead to the dissolution of the Soviet Union.

The New Russia

On December 25, 1991, Gorbachev resigned as president of the Soviet Union. On the same date, the Soviet Union was formally dissolved. In its place, the Commonwealth of Independent States (CIS) was formed. The former Soviet republics were invited to join the CIS, where they would be treated as independent countries with common bonds in the areas of economy and defense. Boris Yeltsin, who was president of the Russian Republic, took control of the former Soviet Union's government.

Boris Yeltsin was the first Russian leader to be elected by the people. Initially, he was a popular leader. Yeltsin's star quickly began to fade, however, when he was faced with the monumental task of transforming Russia. In particular, Russia's transition to a free-market economy and a war for independence in the republic of Chechnya created many problems. Nonetheless, Yeltsin was reelected to a second term as president in 1996.

On December 31, 1999, Yeltsin resigned from office. He appointed Vladimir Putin as his successor. In March 2000, the people of Russia elected Putin as their president. Under his leadership, Russia has developed friendlier relations with both the United States and Europe.

Russia's People Today

Russia's current population includes a diverse mix of ethnic Russians and people from a wide variety of minority ethnic groups. About 82 percent of the people living in Russia today are ethnic Russians—descendants of the original Slavs who settled in

Current Russian president Vladimir Putin was a KGB officer stationed in Germany from 1975 until 1991. After the Soviet collapse, he was the head of the FSB (which replaced the KGB) from 1998 to 1999.

Kievan Rus. The other 18 percent of the population is widely dispersed among roughly 100 ethnic groups.

After ethnic Russians, the next largest ethnic group is the Tatars. In addition to living in Russia, many Tatars live in Ukraine and Uzbekistan. The Tatars are descendants of the Mongol people who invaded Russia in the thirteenth century. They speak a Turkic language and follow the religion of Islam. The Bashkirs and Chuvash are two other minority ethnic groups living in Russia that are also of Mongol ancestry. Like the Tatars, most Bashkirs follow Islam. Most Chuvash, however, practice Christianity.

A number of Russia's small ethnic groups brave the harsh climate of Siberia. These groups include the Yakut, Inuit, Aleut, and Chukchi. Some of Siberia's inhabitants are nomadic people, meaning that they don't maintain permanent homes but rather move from place to place. Some members of these groups, including the Yakut and the Chukchi, are reindeer herders.

A Nenets woman holds up her baby while her young daughter displays her dog. The Nenets, an ethnic group, follow herds of reindeer, a major food source, into the upper Arctic.

THE LANGUAGES OF RUSSIA

3

Modern-day Russia is home to people from about 100 different ethnic groups, most of which have their own language. During the time of Soviet rule, the Communist government wanted everyone to speak the same language. Consequently, many people in Russia speak the language of their particular ethnic group as well as the shared language of Russian.

The official language of Russia is Russian. It is the most commonly spoken language in the country. It is also used as a second language in many of the other former Soviet republics that returned to their native ethnic languages following independence. In addition to Russian, other Slavic languages such as Ukrainian and Belarusian are widely spoken in Russia. English is also becoming more common.

Russian

More than 150 million people throughout the world speak Russian as their native language. It's the third most common language spoken in Europe, following English and Spanish. Russian is one of only six official languages used by the United Nations.

Russian, also known as Great Russian, is a very old Slavic language. It is part of the eastern branch of the Slavic family of languages. The other two languages

At left, a colored wax tablet from AD 1020 shows the Psalms of David written in Cyrillic. These tablets were found in Novgorod. They are the oldest record of Russian writing. Above, St. Petersburg residents take a break to read the newspaper.

Everyday Words and Phrases

English	Russian	Russian Pronunciation
yes	da	DAH
no	nyet	nee-ET
hello	zdravstvuite	ZDRAST-voo-yet-eh
good-bye	da svidanie	das-vee-DAHN-ya
please	pozhaluista	pa-ZAHL-oos-ta
thank you	spasibo	spah-SEE-bo
mother	mat'	MAHT
father	atyets	ah-TYETS
grandmother	babushka	BAH-boosh-kah
grandfather	dyedushka	DZYAH-doosh-kah
sister	syestra	seh-STRAH
brother	brat	BRAHT

that comprise this branch are Ukrainian (Little Russian) and Belarusian (White Russian). Russian is similar to other Slavic languages, including Czech, Polish, and Bulgarian.

There are three main Russian dialects —northern, southern, and central. The northern Russian dialect extends from St. Petersburg eastward across Siberia. The southern dialect is found in the majority of central and southern Russia. The central dialect occurs in the area between the northern and southern dialects, particularly in the city of Moscow and surrounding areas. Modern literary Russian is based on this central dialect.

The Russian language looks and sounds very different from English, and English-speaking people often find it difficult to learn. A few Russian words, including czar, vodka, and samovar, have been adopted into the English language.

Cyrillic Alphabet

In the ninth century, Saint Cyril and his brother, Saint Methodius, served as missionaries from the Roman Catholic Church. They served among the Slavic people, setting out to convert them to Christianity. The two missionaries wanted to provide a written language so that the Slavs could read the Bible. Cyril and Methodius created a new alphabet by adapting the Greek alphabet. Then they used this new alphabet, known as the Glagolithic alphabet, to translate the Bible into the

Saint Cyril and his brother (*right*) believed that people should be allowed to worship in their own native language.

languages used by the Slavs. The Glagolithic alphabet was later modified and renamed the Cyrillic alphabet after Saint Cyril, who was the more literary of the two brothers. Today, the Cyrillic alphabet is still used to write the Russian language.

Because the Cyrillic alphabet is based on the Greek alphabet, it is not at all like English, which is based on the Roman alphabet. The Cyrillic alphabet consists of thirty-three letters, many of which don't resemble any letters in the Roman alphabet. It has about twelve additional letters that were invented to represent Slavic sounds not found in the Greek alphabet. The letters in the Cyrillic alphabet correspond to all of the consonants and vowels used in spoken Russian. The Ukrainian, Bulgarian, and Serbian languages also use modified versions of the Cyrillic alphabet.

Old Church Slavonic

Old Church Slavonic was the first Slavic literary language. All of

The early Cyrillic alphabet was developed during the tenth century in Bulgaria. Early Cyrillic was eventually replaced by the modern Cyrillic alphabet over the next few hundred years.

The last front page of the newspaper *Pravda*, from March 13, 1991. *Pravda* (Truth) was a publication of the Soviet Communist Party. It was first published in 1912 and officially shut down by Boris Yelstin in 1991.

the Slavic languages, including Russian, most likely developed from it. Many contemporary Russian words have their origins in Old Church Slavonic, which is the language of the Russian Orthodox Church. The oldest manuscripts in Russia were written mainly in Old Church Slavonic.

By the eighteenth century, literature in Russia was being written in the Russian language. In the nineteenth century, the work of poet Aleksandr Pushkin helped to improve and refine the Russian literary language. His writings combined the formal Old Church Slavonic style with the informal Russian style. Eventually, the Russian language completely replaced Old Church Slavonic except for religious use within the Russian Orthodox Church.

Other Languages

While Russian is by far the most widely spoken language in Russia, many ethnic minority groups speak other languages. The people of Russia can be divided into four distinct

A city bus in St. Petersburg. The bus is a popular mode of transportation for Russians. Long-distance buses connect to more smaller cities and villages than do trains or planes.

language groups: the East Slavs, the Altaic group, the Uralic group, and the Caucasian group. The largest of these groups is the East Slavs, of which the majority are Russians but also includes Ukrainians and Belarusians. Many members of the Altaic group, including Tatars, Chuvash, and Bashkir, speak various Turkic languages. Some in the Altaic group speak Mongolian. The Uralic group, named for the Ural Mountains, speaks Finno-Ugric and Samoyedic languages. The Caucasian group, named for the Caucasus Mountains, speaks a variety of northwest and northeast Caucasian languages.

In addition to these primary languages, Russian children study a foreign language in school. English is the most popular choice of Russian students. Beginning as early as kindergarten, students study the language by listening to spoken English. It is considered an important language to learn because English is spoken in many countries throughout the world. Knowing English may help Russian students when they pursue a career later in life.

A list of rules and regulations for visitors to the Peter and Paul Fortress in St. Petersburg. Some of the rules include: no skiing, no drinking, no dogs, and no naked potbellies.

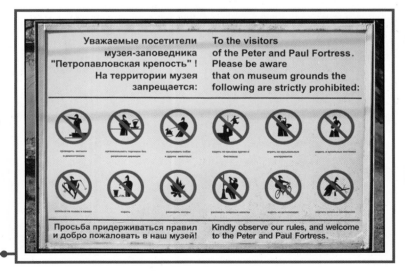

RUSSIAN MYTHS AND LEGENDS

4

U nlike many other cultures, Russians don't have a history of complex myths about gods and goddesses, epic narratives, or ancient holy books. Instead, most Russian myths and legends are folktales and fairy tales passed down from generation to generation. While some are geared specifically toward children, many Russian folktales are popular with people of all age groups.

The world of Russian folktales is populated with beautiful maidens, brave heroes, wicked witches, evil sorcerers, and mythical creatures with magic powers. Many of the stories focus on the classic struggle between good and evil, with good eventually triumphing over evil. Other Russian tales involve various aspects of nature, such as the sun and moon, the four seasons, and the four elements (water, air, earth, and fire). Additional themes include basic concepts such as family, values, human nature, and basic human needs.

Vasilisa and Baba Yaga

The characters of Vasilisa and Baba Yaga appear in several Russian folktales—sometimes together and sometimes separately. Often portrayed as a princess,

At left is an illustration from the *Tale of Ivan Tsarevitch: The Firebird and the Grey Wolf*. This illustration was completed in 1901. It was drawn by artist Ivan Jakovlevitch Bilibin. Above is an illustration for the story "Baba the Witch." This picture was published in a 1915 collection of fairy tales called *Old Peter's Russian Tales*.

Vasilisa is always the heroine in these stories. She is alternately known as Vasilisa the Beautiful, Vasilisa the Wise, or Vasilisa the Brave. At the opposite end of the spectrum is Baba Yaga, an evil witch who is said to eat human flesh. Sometimes called Bony Legs, Baba Yaga lives in a wooden hut set on giant chicken's feet or hen's feet. Surrounding the hut is a fence made of human bones and topped with human skulls that have glowing eyes.

"Vasilisa the Beautiful"

One of the most well-known Russian folktales, "Vasilisa the Beautiful" involves both Vasilisa and Baba Yaga. In the story, Vasilisa lives with her father, her cruel stepmother, and her wretched stepsisters. One day, the stepsisters send Vasilisa to Baba Yaga's house to fetch a light in the middle of the night. Although Baba Yaga tries to eat the fair Vasilisa, the young girl uses a magic doll to pass Baba Yaga's tests, outsmart the witch, and escape. She takes one of the glowing skulls from Baba Yaga's fence for light and returns home to her stepmother and stepsisters. But when they snatch the light from Vasilisa, the glowing eyes of the skull burn into the stepmother and stepsisters, turning them to ashes. Vasilisa is not hurt by the skull's glowing eyes, and she and her father live happily ever after.

"The Frog Princess"

The character of Vasilisa also appears in "The Frog Princess." In

An 1899 illustration by Ivan Bilibin depicts Vasilisa wandering in the forest. Vasilisa is the fairy-tale heroine of the folktale "Vasilisa the Beautiful."

this story, a czar tells each of his three sons to shoot his bow and arrow as far as he can. Whoever finds the arrow will marry the prince who shot it. The arrows of the two older sons are found by lovely maidens from wealthy families. The youngest son, Prince Ivan, is not so lucky. When he finally finds his arrow, it's in the mouth of a frog. Following their father's orders, the two older sons marry the lovely maidens and Prince Ivan marries the frog!

To test the skills of his sons' wives, the czar has the new brides perform several household chores. Unknown to Prince Ivan, his frog wife is actually Princess Vasilisa. Each night, she sheds her frog skin and completes the czar's tasks, doing a much better job than the other two brothers' wives. When the czar holds a grand ball, Princess Vasilisa appears as herself, instead of as a frog. Prince Ivan is thrilled to discover that he is married to the beautiful Princess Vasilisa. Before she can explain her story, Prince Ivan throws her frog skin into the fire, thinking that burning the skin will keep her from turning back into a frog.

As it turns out, though, Vasilisa is under an evil curse. If Prince Ivan had waited three more days, she would have stayed a princess forever. Instead, Vasilisa becomes a prisoner of the wicked Koschei the Invincible. Prince Ivan must then pass a series of tests in order to find his princess, defeat the evil Koschei, and break the curse on Vasilisa.

"The Firebird"

In Russian folklore, there are several versions of "The Firebird." One version was even turned into a ballet, with music by the famous Russian composer Igor Stravinsky. In that version of the story, Prince Ivan encounters the firebird while on a hunting trip. Ivan decides to spare the firebird's life when the colorful bird offers him a gift—a magic feather from its tail.

As Prince Ivan continues on his journey, he comes upon an enchanted castle. In the castle's courtyard are ten lovely maidens. The maidens warn Ivan about the evil Koschei the Invincible, who lives in the castle and holds them captive. For his own amusement, Koschei turns all visitors into stone. Determined to rescue the maidens, Prince Ivan enters the castle to face the evil Koschei. The firebird's feather protects Ivan from Koschei and his ogres, and soon, the firebird itself arrives and helps Ivan destroy all the evil beings. Upon Koschei's death, his spell is broken and the people who had been turned to stone return to their human

An illustration by Ivan Bilibin depicts Ivan taking a tail feather from the mystical firebird. This illustration is from the 1901 *Tale of Ivan Tsarevitch: The Firebird and the Grey Wolf.*

forms. Prince Ivan wins the hand of the loveliest maiden, who turns out to be a princess.

"The Giant Turnip"

"The Giant Turnip" is a popular Russian folktale for children. Many years ago, turnips were a common vegetable in Russian cooking. In translations for American readers, the turnip is often replaced with a carrot since carrots are more common in American cooking. The tale may have been first told by traveling Russian minstrels as early as the twelfth century.

In "The Giant Turnip," an old man plants a turnip in his garden. Over time, the turnip grows and grows until it is very large. It's so enormous, in fact, that the old man can't pull it out of the ground by himself. He calls his wife over to help him pull the turnip out of the ground. The two of them pull and pull, but still they can't move the giant turnip. They ask for help from relatives and neighbors, with each person holding on to the person in front. They form a long chain of people pulling and pulling, but still the turnip won't budge. Finally, someone very small—in some versions, a tiny child; in other versions, a mouse—offers to help pull. Although everyone thinks that the child or mouse is too small to make any difference, the giant turnip is finally pulled from the ground with the little one's help. The moral of the story involves the importance of teamwork and not underestimating others.

Snow Maiden

Once upon a time, an elderly peasant couple lived in the forests of Russia. Although the man and woman loved each other, they were unhappy. They had always longed for a child of their own.

One winter day, the couple was watching the neighborhood children build a snowman. Soon, the old man had an idea. "Let's go outside and build a snow child," he said to his wife.

So the couple rolled a big ball of snow for the body and a smaller one for the head. They added arms and legs, eyes, a nose, and a mouth. Then the woman kissed the snow child, and something magical happened. The snow child's eyes began to twinkle, and her mouth curled into a smile. She tilted her head to one side and brushed the snow off her arms and legs. The snow child had come to life in the form of a beautiful girl!

The old man and woman were thrilled! They finally had the child they had always wanted. They named the girl Snow Maiden and took her home to their cottage. Snow Maiden was a sweet and happy girl, and the couple loved her very much. All winter long, Snow Maiden spent much of her time playing in the forest.

As the days grew warmer and spring arrived, Snow Maiden became unhappy. One day, Snow Maiden told the old couple that she had to leave them and return to the land of snow. As she waved good-bye, the couple wept and begged her to stay. It was no use, though. The old man and woman were distraught, fearing that they had lost their daughter forever. All summer long, they remained unhappy.

But when the weather grew cold and the first snow fell, there was a knock at the door. It was Snow Maiden! And so it was that Snow Maiden lived with the old couple every winter and returned to the land of snow every spring.

Based on a Russian folktale

The Legend of Anastasia

One of history's greatest mysteries involves the legend of a real-life princess—Anastasia Romanov, Grand Duchess of Russia. Born in 1901, Anastasia was the youngest daughter of Nicholas II, the last czar of Russia. Nicholas and his wife, Alexandra, had four daughters, Olga, Tatiana, Maria, and Anastasia, and one son, Alexei. Although Alexei was the youngest child, he was the only male heir and, according to tradition, would become the next czar.

Anastasia, Alexei, and their sisters grew up in the luxurious world of royalty. They lived in grand palaces, had private tutors, and studied Russian, German, French, and English. Young Anastasia had a sunny disposition and earned the nickname the Imp because of her impish sense of humor. She often amused family members with her jokes, skits, and funny impressions of palace visitors.

By 1917, when Anastasia was sixteen years old, the political climate in Russia had changed. The common people were fed up with food shortages and other poor conditions in Russia, and they began to riot. By March 1917, the rioting had turned

A 1910 photograph of Nicholas II's daughter Anastasia. Skeptics suggest that the bones of Anastasia and her brother, Alexei, were not found because they were cremated.

into a full-blown revolution. The people would no longer tolerate being ruled by a czar. Czar Nicholas II was forced to abdicate, or give up, the throne and move his family to exile in Siberia.

The Bolsheviks (later called the Communists) then took control of the Russian government. In the spring of 1918, they imprisoned the Romanov family in a house in Ekaterinburg, located in the Ural Mountains. Anastasia was seventeen years old. On July 17, 1918, Bolshevik guards woke the family members in the middle of the night and led them into the basement of the house. The guards then drew their guns and proceeded to execute the entire family.

Soon afterward, rumors began to spread about the fate of the Romanov family. According to the legend, some family members—Anastasia, in particular—had miraculously escaped the execution. Within a short time, several people in the United States and Europe claimed to be Anastasia or one of her siblings. Most were quickly discredited. In 1920, however, a woman named Anna Anderson convinced many people, including several surviving relatives of the royal family, that she was the real Anastasia. When she died in 1984, her true identity remained a mystery.

In 1991, scientists discovered the skeletal remains of the Romanov family. The mystery deepened, however, when the scientists realized that the bones of Anastasia and her younger brother, Alexei, were missing. Had the youngest Romanovs really survived? Was Anna Anderson telling the truth—that she really was Anastasia? One mystery was solved in 1993, when DNA tests proved that Anna Anderson was not Anastasia. But the fates of Anastasia and Alexei Romanov remain a mystery to this day.

RUSSIAN FESTIVALS AND CEREMONIES OF ANTIQUITY AND TODAY

5

In Russia, holidays and festivals are celebrated throughout the year. Most are joyous occasions filled with special feasts and festivities. Some holidays are observed only by the followers of a particular religion. Members of the Russian Orthodox Church, for example, count Easter and Christmas among their holidays. Several national holidays that were introduced during Soviet rule continue to be observed today, although with less formality than in the past.

Religious Holidays

During the Soviet period, which began in 1917, the Communist rulers who took power were atheists (they did not believe in God). The rulers discouraged the Russian people from practicing religion. This meant that the observation of religious holy days was also frowned upon. The Russian people were encouraged instead to embrace Soviet national holidays. With the breakup of the Soviet Union in 1991, however, came the revival of religion. Today, religious holy days are once again observed throughout Russia.

At left, two children hold up a donkey-shaped balloon during St. Petersburg's Winter Festival. Russians welcome the cold weather like an old friend. Above, a young boy eats a tasty pancake in celebration of Maslenitsa. This holiday is also known as Shrovetide.

Russian Orthodox women pray and sing hymns at an Easter service. In the Russian Orthodox Church, Easter is also called the Feast of Feasts or the King of Days. It is the most important holiday of the year for Russian Orthodox Christians.

Easter

Easter is by far the most important holiday in the Russian Orthodox Church. While Easter Sunday falls in early spring, the Easter season actually begins much earlier. In the six weeks before Easter Sunday, most Russian Orthodox Christians observe Lent, when meat and dairy products are eliminated from the diet. In preparation for Lent, Russians celebrate Maslenitsa. Also known as Butter Week, Maslenitsa is a week of festivities and food, especially pancakes loaded with butter. Maslenitsa activities include sledding and snowball fights to usher in the end of winter and the beginning of spring.

Maslenitsa ends with the start of Lent, and Lent ends with Easter. On the night before Easter, Russian Orthodox Christians attend church services. At midnight, the worshippers carry lit candles and follow the priest around the church as they are led in prayer and song. Easter Sunday is a day of feasting. A popular Easter activity for both children and adults is decorating Easter eggs, called *pysanka*. Eggs are painted

A procession of happy people celebrates Christmas in the snow. Many villagers have small community parades like this one to celebrate the holiday.

with elaborate designs and given as gifts. Some people make pysanka with carved wooden eggs rather than real eggs.

Christmas

In the Russian Orthodox Church, Christmas does not fall on December 25. Instead, Christmas is celebrated on January 7. The reason is that the Russian Orthodox Church follows the Julian calendar, started by the Roman emperor Julius Caesar in 46 BC. In many countries, the Julian calendar was replaced with the Gregorian calendar, started by Pope Gregory XIII in 1582. Russia, however, didn't switch until 1918. The Russian Orthodox Church never switched and continues to use the Julian calendar to this day.

Christmas is a fairly solemn religious holiday in Russia. During Soviet rule, people were discouraged from celebrating Christmas. Many of the traditions usually associated with Christmas were then transferred over to New Year's Day. After the Soviet era ended, Russians once again began to celebrate Christmas. But the New Year's traditions stuck, and for most Russians, New Year's Day remains a more festive holiday than Christmas.

Muslim Holy Days

Muslims live throughout Russia but are mostly found near the Volga Basin and in the area between the Black Sea and the Caspian Sea. Muslims observe many holy days throughout the year. Some are solemn occasions for prayer, while others are festive occasions for celebration. Ramadan is considered by many Muslims to be the holiest time of the Muslim year. Rather than being a single day, Ramadan is actually

In Moscow, a New Year's celebration is held for children at the Kremlin Palace of Congresses. These spectacles are held annually and include clowns, actors, and acrobats.

an entire month. Ramadan takes place during the ninth month of the Muslim lunar year. During the month of Ramadan, Muslims are not allowed to eat or drink anything between sunrise and sunset. On the day following the end of Ramadan, Muslims celebrate with a large feast in honor of the breaking of the fast. On this day, Muslims also exchange gifts.

Secular Holidays

Not all Russian holidays celebrate religious occasions. Some Russian holidays are secular, or nonreligious. These secular holidays include New Year's Day and several national holidays.

New Year's Day

In Russia, many Christmas traditions have evolved into New Year's traditions. Rather than decorating a Christmas tree, for example, many Russians decorate a New Year's tree. Instead of receiving gifts from Santa Claus or Saint Nicholas, Russian children are given presents by Grandfather Frost and his helper, the Snow Maiden. The festivities begin with a champagne toast at midnight on New Year's Eve. Then Russian families enjoy a huge feast, which begins just after midnight and continues into the morning hours.

At right, a large-scale parade is held on the first of May in Red Square, Moscow, 1957. The Soviet flag is waved and the square is decorated with large portraits of the Soviet leader Lenin.

In 1957, the Soviet Union celebrated the fortieth anniversary of the Bolshevik Revolution. Above, soldiers carrying large flags march in Red Square. Many parades, ceremonies, and protests have been held in Moscow's Red Square throughout history.

National Holidays

During Soviet rule, a great deal of emphasis was placed on the observance of Soviet national holidays, rather than on religious holidays. Many of these national holidays celebrated events that led to the establishment of the Soviet Union. During the Soviet era, holidays such as Labor Day and October Revolution Day were commemorated with huge parades and pageantry. Thousands of people marched through Moscow's Red Square, carrying banners with pictures of Communist leaders. Since the breakup of the Soviet Union, these holidays have become much less important than in the past. Some are still observed, however.

International Women's Day, celebrated on March 8, is a day when Russians honor the women in their lives. Husbands give flowers and gifts to their wives, and children give gifts to their mothers and female teachers. The first day of May marks the May Day celebration. In Soviet times, it was known as Labor Day and was a huge holiday to honor workers. On May 9, Victory Day is a day of remembrance for the Russian

In Moscow on May 9, 2003, soldiers dress in World War II uniforms to commemorate VE Day, the defeat of Nazi Germany in 1945.

soldiers who fought in World War II. November 7 is the anniversary of the October 1917 revolution that established Communist power.

After Soviet rule ended in 1991, Russians added a new holiday to their calendar, Russia Day. This is an Independence Day holiday celebrated on June 12. It was on that day in 1990 that the Russian Republic formally declared its sovereignty.

Ethnic Festivals

Many Russian ethnic groups observe their own holidays with cultural festivals. Some of these festivals celebrate harvesttime. The Turkic

A Turkic man plays a traditional wind instrument during the Datsan Lamaist Festival. The festival takes place in Shawm, Buryatia.

A group of Komi women and children wear their traditional regional costumes for a festival in Beloyarskii, Siberia. Most Komis live in the northern central part of Russia in a self-governing district called the Komi Republic. The capital of the Komi Republic is Syktyvkar.

ethnic groups, for example, celebrate Sabantui, which means "plow feast." Sabantui is observed after the sowing season is finished but before the hay mowing season has begun. During this time, farmers have a few days for rest. Tatars, Chuvashes, and members of other Turkic ethnic groups take part in a variety of Sabantui festivities, including singing, dancing, and playing games.

Other ethnic festivals commemorate the change of seasons, especially the beginning of spring. The Navruz festival, for example, is celebrated each year on the first day of spring. Navruz, which means "new day," is a time of renewal. During Navruz, people begin again with a clean slate and renewed happiness. It's a time when people put aside their differences and forget their sorrows. Navruz festivities include holiday banquets and the exchange of gifts.

Moscow Circus

It's a cause for celebration when the circus comes to town! For more than 200 years, the Moscow Circus has thrilled audiences with its world-renowned acts. The circus goes on tour every year, performing in both large cities and small towns throughout Russia. The Russian troupes execute daring acrobatic moves on a tightrope, on a trapeze, and on horseback. Clowns perform silly stunts and juggling tricks to make the audience laugh. Crowd favorites include the many animals, such as elephants, monkeys, and bears, trained to perform a variety of stunts.

The Moscow Circus draws crowds on its opening night at Madison Square Garden in New York City. The Moscow Circus has many acts involving elephants, bears, horses, and tigers. The circus is a family business. Many trainers and performers are part of the same family.

THE RELIGIONS OF RUSSIA THROUGHOUT ITS HISTORY

6

*Religion is the sigh of the oppressed creature, the heart
of a heartless world, and the soul of soulless conditions.
It is the opium of the people.*

—Karl Marx (1818–1883)

R eligion in Russia has had its share of ups and downs throughout history. After the Russian Revolution in 1917, the new Communist government declared that the Soviet Union was an atheist country. The Russian people were strongly discouraged from practicing any religion. Churches did not receive

any government support, and many were closed. Religious holidays and festivals were outlawed and replaced with national government holidays and parades. Soviet citizens caught worshipping in public could be arrested or lose their jobs.

Starting in the late 1980s, the Soviet government once again began to allow religious worship. Following the fall of Communism, all Russians were granted complete religious freedom. Although the majority of people living in Russia today follow the Russian Orthodox faith, many other religions are also practiced. These include other denominations of Christianity, Islam, Judaism, and Buddhism.

At left is a fifteenth-century depiction of the archangel Michael by Andrei Rublev. During his lifetime, Rublev was the foremost iconic painter for the Russian Orthodox Church. Above is St. Sergius, the grand monastery of Zagorsk. The monastery was founded in the fourteenth century.

Christianity

Christianity is a religion based on the life and teachings of Jesus Christ and on the Bible as the holy book. Followers of Christianity are generally members of one of three main groups: Roman Catholic, Eastern Orthodox, or Protestant. Although these groups have different beliefs about Jesus, most Christians believe that Jesus was the son of God and that God sent Jesus as the savior. Christianity is the largest religion in the world, with about 2 billion followers around the globe. In Russia, the majority of Christians belong to the Russian Orthodox Church.

Russian Orthodoxy

When Christianity was first introduced in Russia, the country's Christian churches were led by Constantinople's head priest, known as the patriarch. During that time, Constantinople (modern-day Istanbul, Turkey) was the capital of the Byzantine Empire. By the fifteenth century, however, Russian churches were being led by their own Russian patriarch. Since then, they have been known as the Russian Orthodox Church. Since 1990, the patriarch of the Russian Orthodox Church has been Alexy II. In the Russian Orthodox Church, the patriarch holds a position similar to the pope in the Roman Catholic Church.

At one time the nation's official religion, Russian Orthodoxy remains far and away the most practiced religion in Russia. Along with the Greek Orthodox

The Orthodox patriarch, Alexy II, performs a ceremony at Nikolaugrieski Monastery. Alexy II is the fifteenth leader of the Russian Orthodox Church.

The Assumption Cathedral in Moscow was commissioned in 1475 by Ivan III. Its onion-shaped domes are typical of the Russian Orthodox architectural style. This cathedral was designed by Aristotele Fioravanti. It was completed in 1479.

religion, the Russian Orthodox faith is part of the Eastern Orthodox branch of Christianity. Although the Eastern Orthodox religions share many common beliefs with Roman Catholics, they also have many differences.

With their onion-shaped domes, often painted in gold, Russian Orthodox churches are easy to recognize from the outside. The inside of a Russian Orthodox church is elaborately decorated with religious art. Burning candles light up the interior, and burning incense scents the air. An altar is located at the center of the church sanctuary. An ornate altar screen, called an iconostasis, separates the sanctuary from the rest of the church. Special doors in the center of the iconostasis, called the royal gates, enable the priest to enter and leave the main room of the church. Only the priest is allowed to walk through these doors. The congregation views the sanctuary through the royal gates.

A funeral service at Preobrojensky Orthodox Church in St. Petersburg. Mourners stand and pray over the deceased while the priest delivers a eulogy.

Church Services

Russian Orthodox services are generally formal, solemn occasions. During a church service, worshippers stand or kneel facing the iconostasis. There is no seating inside the church. Rather than speaking, the priest sings or chants in Russian throughout the service. At times, he may sprinkle holy water over the congregation.

Russian Orthodox church services include the Divine Liturgy, the Divine Office, and Occasional Offices. The Divine Liturgy is the sacrament of the Eucharist, which is performed by both the priest and the worshippers. The Divine Office includes prayers and readings, which are called matins and vespers. Occasional Offices include sacraments and services for marriages, baptisms, and funerals.

Sacraments

A sacrament is a Christian rite or observance. The Russian Orthodox Church administers seven major sacraments:

Baptism When a child is born, a baptism is performed to allow the infant into the church. A baptism can also be performed on a person who converts to the Russian Orthodox religion. During the ceremony, a priest submerges the person who is being baptized into water three times and then blesses the individual.

Confirmation Immediately following a baptism, confirmation is administered to give the baptized individual full church membership. Confirmation also provides the right to take part in the Eucharist.

Eucharist In this sacrament, worshippers take Holy Communion, when they receive bread and wine that represent the body and blood of Jesus Christ. The Eucharist is a remembrance of Christ's victory over death, shared by the faithful.

Confession In front of a priest, a person confesses his or her sins to God. The person's sins are forgiven by the priest in the name of God.

Marriage In the Russian Orthodox Church, marriage is a sacrament that joins a man and woman together and forms a family. The church allows divorce and remarriage but believes that the first marriage is the greatest in God's eyes.

Anointing of the Sick If a person is ill, a priest may administer this sacrament. The priest prays for the person's recovery and for forgiveness of his or her sins.

Holy Orders This sacrament admits men into the clergy. A new priest can be ordained only by a bishop, however.

Three couples are wed at the Church of the Archangel Michael in Novokuznetsk. In Russia, weddings last anywhere from two days to a whole week. According to Russian tradition, the longer the guests stay, the closer the friendship.

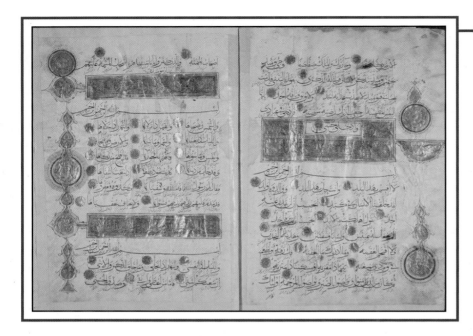

A thirteenth-century, decorative page from the Koran. Each of the swirl designs represents a new verse or chapter.

Islam

Islam is one of the world's major religions. In Russia, an estimated 15 to 20 million people—or 10 to 15 percent of the Russian population—follow the faith of Islam. It's the second-largest religion after Russian Orthodoxy.

Islam is an Arabic word that means "surrender to the will of Allah (God)." The prophet Muhammad started Islam sometime after AD 600. A follower of Islam is called a Muslim, which means "one who surrenders (to Allah)." Muslims believe that Allah revealed the divine word to Muhammad. These revelations were recorded in the Koran—the Muslim holy book. The Koran forbids lying, stealing, and murder, and teaches virtues such as honesty, kindness, and charity. Muslims submit to Allah by performing the duties outlined in the Five Pillars of Islam:

Faith Becoming a Muslim requires a profession of faith in Allah and Muhammad. A person must state his or her belief that there is only one God and that Muhammad was a prophet of God.

Prayer Muslims pray five times daily—at sunrise, at noon, in the afternoon, in the evening, and at sundown. Every Friday, Muslims gather together to pray at a Muslim house of worship, known as a mosque.

Charity Muslims believe in the importance of charity, or helping those less fortunate. Muslims are expected to give regular donations to the poor, called a *zakat*.

Fasting During Ramadan, Muslims fast during the hours between dawn and dusk. A three-day celebration marks the end of Ramadan.

Pilgrimage All able Muslims are required to make a pilgrimage to Mecca at least once during their lifetime. This pilgrimage is known as the *hajj*.

In the Republic of Daghestan, Muslim men pray at the central mosque. Over thirty different ethnic groups reside in Daghestan. It is one of Russia's most diverse republics. The largest ethnic groups are Avars, Darghins, and Lezghins. Most people living in Daghestan are Muslim.

The three holiest places in Islam are Mecca, Medina, and Jerusalem. Mecca, located in modern-day Saudi Arabia, is the holiest city because it's the birthplace of Muhammad. Muslims face Mecca during prayer. Medina, also in modern-day Saudi Arabia, is the second holiest city. Muhammad fled to Medina—after being driven out of Mecca—and was welcomed by the people there. Medina is also the place where Muhammad is buried. Jerusalem, found in modern-day Israel, is the third

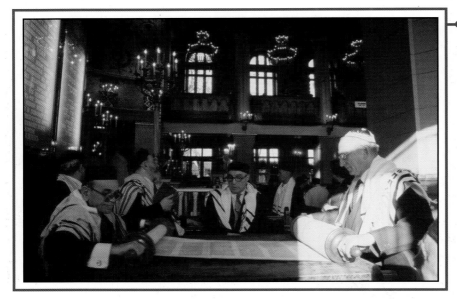

Jewish leaders unroll scrolls of scripture at a Russian synagogue. Since the collapse of the Soviet Union, over 1 million Russian Jews have immigrated to Israel and the United States.

holiest city because it's home to the Dome of the Rock, a Muslim shrine. Muslims believe that Muhammad ascended to heaven to receive God's commandments at this site.

Islam has two main sects: Sunni and Shiite. In Russia, the majority of Muslims are members of the Sunni sect. They are mainly Turkic people living near the Volga River and in the region between the Black Sea and Caspian Sea. Russia has thousands of mosques.

Judaism

Judaism is the religious beliefs and practices of the Jews. In the days of the czars, several million Jews lived in Russia. They were often persecuted for their religious beliefs, however, and many immigrated to the United States. Under Soviet rule, the persecution continued, although in more subtle ways. The Jewish people were assigned to live in an isolated area of eastern Siberia, but most continued to live in western Russia.

Beginning in the late 1980s—when Communist restrictions were eased and people were allowed to leave Russia—many more Jews moved to Israel or the United States. Today, it's estimated that fewer than 500,000 Jews are living in Russia. There are synagogues, where Jewish people worship, in all the major Russian cities. St. Petersburg is home to one of the largest synagogues in Europe.

Buddhism

In addition to Christians, Muslims, and Jews, Russia is also home to many Buddhists. Buddhism was founded in India around 500 BC by a teacher called Buddha, which means "the enlightened one." Buddhists have three main beliefs, which they refer to as the Three Refuges: the Buddha himself; the dharma, which are the Buddha's teachings; and the sangha, which is the religious community he founded.

A group of Lamaist monks practice their beliefs at a monastery in Ulan Ude in Buryatia. Lamaist Buddhism is also called Tibetan Buddhism. The head of Tibetan Buddhism is the Dalai Lama, who is believed to be a reincarnation of the Buddha of Compassion.

With about 350 million followers worldwide, Buddhism is another of the world's major religions. The majority of Buddhists live in Southeast Asia, Japan, and Sri Lanka. In Russia, about 300,000 people follow the Buddhist faith. Most Russian Buddhists live in cities such as St. Petersburg and Moscow or in the Tuva, Huryat, or Kalmyk republics.

THE ART AND ARCHITECTURE OF RUSSIA

7

A rt and architecture have been prominent in Russia since the country was founded. Before the twentieth century, Russian art and architecture were influenced mainly by religion. Around AD 988, the ruler of Kievan Rus—Prince Vladimir—was converted to Christianity. Specifically, he embraced the Byzantine faith (which later became the Eastern Orthodox Church) and adopted it as the religion of the Russian state. Much of the early art and architecture in Russia, particularly in Moscow, reflects this Byzantine style. Western European influences can be seen in Russia's art and architectural styles from later years.

Religious Painting

Russia has a long tradition of religious painting. Russian artists adorned the interiors of churches with mosaics and frescoes of religious subject matter. They also created many icons, which are traditional religious paintings considered holy by the Eastern Orthodox Church. Icons, which are often painted on small wooden panels, usually portray images of Jesus Christ, the Virgin Mary, or saints. Because they are meant to show the heavenly glory of these sacred figures, icons are purposely created to not look like realistic portraits. Instead, artists used rich colors and gold leaf to create flat, stylized images.

At left is the painting *The Street in the Village* (1976) by Marc Chagall. Some of Chagall's major works are *I and the Village* (1911), *The Birthday* (1915), *Green Violinist* (1923–1924), and *Solitude* (1933). Above is a seventeenth-century Russian icon painting. It depicts Mary holding the infant Jesus.

Transverse Line (1923) by Wassily Kandinsky. One of the largest collections of Kandinsky's paintings is at the Guggenheim Museum in New York City.

Modern Painting

By the second half of the nineteenth century, Russia had thriving art schools. Russian artists were beginning to choose subjects beyond the scope of religion. Just before World War I began in 1914, more Russian artists began to emerge. Although Russia has produced many well-respected contemporary artists, two modern painters are among the most famous—Wassily Kandinsky and Marc Chagall.

Wassily Kandinsky (1866–1944) was born in Moscow. He is generally considered the father of abstraction in modern painting. Abstract artists don't try to create realistic art. Although Kandinsky studied law and economics at the University of Moscow, art was his true calling. In 1896, he made a leap of faith and moved to Munich, Germany, to study art and become a painter. There, he and German painter Franz Marc founded der Blaue Reiter (The Blue Rider), an expressionist art movement, in 1911. At the start of World War I, Kandinsky returned to Russia. During that time, he continued to paint and also taught art at the Moscow Academy of Fine Arts. In 1921, he left Russia once again and moved to Berlin, Germany. During World War II, he left Berlin and lived out the remainder of his life in Paris. Kandinsky's paintings had a profound influence on twentieth-century art.

A 1960s photograph of Marc Chagall at his home in St.-Paul de Vence, France. Chagall was buried near his house in the St.-Paul town cemetery.

Marc Chagall (1887–1985) was born in Vitebsk, Russia (now part of Belarus). He was raised in a devoutly Jewish family. After moving from Russia to Paris in 1910, Chagall started to include childhood memories and religious symbols in his paintings. This work included his recollections of Jewish life in Russian villages. His artistic style reflected the influence of cubism and surrealism. Cubism was a modern art movement that began in France in the early 1900s. Cubist painters represented objects in nature in terms of basic geometric shapes. Surrealism was another modern art movement, started in Paris in the 1920s, in which artists explored human nature through the world of dreams and fantasy. Although Chagall returned to Russia for a few years, he left his homeland for good in 1922. He lived most of his life in France but also spent several years in the United States during World War II.

Sculpture

Many Russian sculptures are monuments dedicated to Russia's leaders. These monuments were created in the likenesses of Peter the Great, Catherine the Great, and other beloved Russian czars. During the Soviet era, sculptures of Vladimir Lenin, Joseph Stalin, and other Communist leaders adorned public areas. Other statues commemorate war heroes and victories in battle. Most recently, sculptures of famous Russian literary figures have been unveiled.

One of Russia's most well-known sculptures—and the one that is most often used to symbolize Russia—is located in Volgograd (formerly Stalingrad). Known as *Mother Russia,* this enormous outdoor statue is the

The sculpture *Mother Russia* is located on top of Mamal Hill, a battle site during the Battle of Stalingrad. *Mother Russia* is the focal point of Mamayev Kurgan Museum, which commemorates the Battle of Stalingrad.

A 1920 collage entitled *The Construction of the USSR* by photographer Alexander Rodchenko. Rodchenko believed his work represented the spirit of the revolution.

central focus of a World War II memorial complex. The sculpture depicts a woman with a raised sword guarding her country. Completed in 1967, *Mother Russia* is constructed of 5,500 tons (4,990 metric tons) of concrete and stands 171 feet (52 m) high—20 feet (6 m) taller than the Statue of Liberty.

Poster Art

During the Soviet era, the Communist government did not want artwork to reflect an artist's personal ideas or style. Creativity and individuality were discouraged, and some Russian artists moved to Europe or North America to enjoy freedom of expression. The Soviet government wanted all artwork to depict respected Communist leaders and happy, faithful citizens and workers. Soviet art was intended to encourage people to support Communism and persuade them to be happy with their day-to-day existence, despite its hardships.

The most common type of art created during the Soviet period was the Communist propaganda poster. These posters typically glorified Communism and its leaders. They were often displayed on public buildings or carried through city streets during military parades and on Soviet national holidays.

Folk Art

Folk art is a very old tradition in Russia. For centuries, Russian craftspeople have been creating beautiful folk

A set of *matryoshkas* (Russian nesting dolls). Some artists paint scenes or expressions on their matryoshkas that tell a popular folktale or fable.

Fabergé Eggs

One of the most exquisite artistic legacies of the Russian czars is the Fabergé egg. In the Russian Orthodox Church, Easter is the most important holiday. During the Easter celebration, a Russian tradition is to give decorated eggs as gifts. In 1885, Czar Alexander III wanted to give his wife a very special Easter gift because it was the year of their twentieth wedding anniversary. The czar ordered a special egg to be designed by Peter Carl Fabergé, a talented jeweler.

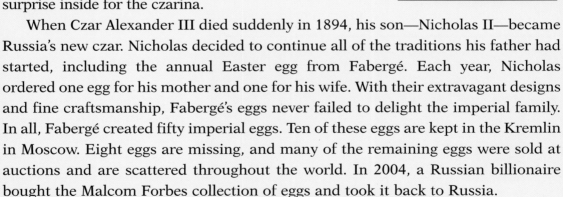

From the outside, the egg that Fabergé created looked to be a fairly simple enameled egg. Opening the egg, however, revealed a golden yolk. Within the yolk was a golden hen. Inside the hen was a miniature replica of the royal crown and a tiny ruby egg. The czarina was delighted with Fabergé's creation, and the czar commissioned the jeweler to design a new Easter egg every year. The czar specified that each egg must be unique and must hold a surprise inside for the czarina.

When Czar Alexander III died suddenly in 1894, his son—Nicholas II—became Russia's new czar. Nicholas decided to continue all of the traditions his father had started, including the annual Easter egg from Fabergé. Each year, Nicholas ordered one egg for his mother and one for his wife. With their extravagant designs and fine craftsmanship, Fabergé's eggs never failed to delight the imperial family. In all, Fabergé created fifty imperial eggs. Ten of these eggs are kept in the Kremlin in Moscow. Eight eggs are missing, and many of the remaining eggs were sold at auctions and are scattered throughout the world. In 2004, a Russian billionaire bought the Malcom Forbes collection of eggs and took it back to Russia.

art, such as dolls, toys, games, and clothing. They use natural materials found locally, including wood, bark, wool, and clay.

One of the most popular types of Russian folk art, especially with tourists, is the *matryoshka*. These dolls are made in sets, ranging in size from large to small, with each doll fitting inside another doll in the set. They are painted to look like people and then are coated in a clear, shiny lacquer finish. Original matryoshka were painted to resemble traditional Russian women wearing kerchiefs. Now matryoshka are created in many different designs, including Russian czars, Soviet leaders, sports figures, and musical groups. The same painting techniques used for matryoshka are also used to paint decorative wooden boxes and wooden eggs. The boxes are often painted with scenes from Russian folktales.

A great deal of Russian folk art is also created out of fabric. Some Russian ethnic groups make ceremonial clothing with colorful designs, detailed embroidery, and elaborate beadwork. This handmade clothing becomes a work of art. Other types of fabric art include table linens, wall hangings, and rugs.

Architecture

Many of Russia's most impressive architectural achievements can be found in Moscow and St. Petersburg. In addition to beautiful Byzantine-style churches, these cities are home to grand palaces built by Russian czars and world-famous museums. During the Soviet era, the Communist government destroyed many churches in its attempt to outlaw the practicing of religion. During the 1990s—after the fall of Communism—replicas of several of these demolished churches were built.

Churches

For hundreds of years, the buildings in Russia with the most significant architecture were Russian Orthodox churches. Designed in the Byzantine style, these churches are distinguished by their

Catherine the Great's lavish Winter Palace in St. Petersburg. The palace is gigantic. It has 1,786 doors, 1,945 windows, and 1,057 halls and rooms!

unique onion-shaped domes. Russia's most famous Byzantine church is St. Basil's Cathedral in Moscow. Commissioned by Ivan the Terrible, St. Basil's Cathedral was built on the edge of Red Square between 1555 and 1561. According to legend, Ivan the Terrible ordered that the architect be blinded upon completion of the church. Supposedly, the czar didn't want the architect to ever design another building that might rival the beauty of St. Basil's.

Palaces

Russia is home to a large number of grand palaces, most of which were built as residences for the Russian imperial family. Today, many of these palaces have been turned into art or historical museums for the public to enjoy. Other palaces are now used for government functions.

The Kremlin, located at the center of Moscow, is one of Russia's most famous sites. *Kremlin* is a Russian word meaning "fortress" or "citadel." Rather than being just one building, the Kremlin is actually a complex of many structures built at different times and in several different architectural styles. The Kremlin includes palaces, churches, the Duma building, and a bell tower. At the heart of the Kremlin complex is the Grand Kremlin Palace. With more than 700 rooms, the massive yellow-and-white structure was designed to highlight the importance of the Russian imperial family. Originally built as a residence for the czars, the Grand Kremlin Palace is now used for state receptions and official ceremonies.

Museums

Many of Russia's museums are acclaimed not only for their comprehensive collections, but also for their striking architecture. Two

A view of the Kremlin from the Moskva River. Most of the buildings in the Kremlin were built between 1450 and 1850.

The Hermitage Museum at the Winter Palace. Catherine the Great began the collection in 1764 when she purchased 250 paintings for the palace.

such museums are the Hermitage, located in St. Petersburg, and the State Historical Museum in Moscow.

The Hermitage Museum is one of the most famous art museums in the world. The Hermitage collection includes works from such legendary artists as Michelangelo, Leonardo da Vinci, Raphael, Rembrandt, Claude Monet, Paul Cézanne, and Vincent van Gogh. Completed in 1762, the main building of the Hermitage was formerly known as the Winter Palace and was the winter home of the Russian czars. Designed in the baroque architectural style, the green-and-white building has three stories and more than 1,000 lavishly decorated rooms and hallways.

The State Historical Museum, located at the western edge of Moscow's Red Square, charts the history of Russia. Constructed between 1875 and 1881, the museum is an immense red brick building. The museum's architectural elements

include ornamental turrets, decorative cornices, and pinnacles. The building's elaborately decorated interior features murals, ceiling paintings, and wood carvings.

The State Historical Museum is located in Moscow's Red Square. The museum encompasses seven different branches including cathedrals and galleries. The collections are dedicated solely to Russian art, culture, and history.

Soviet Buildings

Most of the architecture from the Soviet period consists of functional buildings with minimal ornamentation. The Soviet government did, however, build a few noteworthy structures, including the Museum of Cosmonautics and the Moscow metro.

Moscow metro stations were designed and embellished by prominent Russian architects, painters, and sculptors. There are over 150 stations in the subway system.

The Museum of Cosmonautics, located in Moscow, highlights the history of Russian space exploration from its early days to the present. The museum is located at the base of a soaring monument entitled *To the Conquerors of Space*. Built in 1964, the monument celebrates the launch of *Sputnik*, the first artificial satellite. The monument features a silver rocket riding atop a titanium obelisk that rises 328 feet (100 m) into the sky.

The Moscow metro is much more than just a subway system. The subway stations, built during the Stalin era, are often referred to as "the people's palaces." The elegantly designed metro stations are filled with marble columns and benches, chandeliers, intricate mosaics, and bronze sculptures. Much of the interior artwork features Soviet leaders and workers.

THE LITERATURE AND MUSIC OF RUSSIA

8

Much like its artistic heritage, Russia's literary heritage began with religious works. Monks, who wrote about the lives of the saints, did the earliest writing in Russia. In the nineteenth century, the Russian czars encouraged greater contact with Europe. During this time, Russian writers began to write about the real world and their opinions about life in Russia. Some of these writers were exiled when their work cast a negative light on Russian nobility. During the twentieth century—when the Soviet government was in power—many talented Russian writers left the country to avoid Communist control over their work. Of those who remained, however, several won the prestigious Nobel Prize for Literature.

Until the mid-eighteenth century, most Russian music was also of a religious nature. It was vocal music sung during church services. Beginning in 1741, with the reign of Empress Elizabeth, secular (nonreligious) music became popular in Russia. The popularity of classical music continued throughout the eighteenth century, with the reign of Catherine the Great. In the nineteenth and twentieth centuries, several Russian composers received international recognition for their work. During this same time, Russian ballet also became world famous.

At left is a collection of notes for Pyotr Ilich Tchaikovsky's (1840–1893) opera *The Queen of Spades* (1890). Tchaikovsky composed ten operas. The majority of Tchaikovsky's compositions, however, are orchestral and chamber works. Above is an 1827 painting of Aleksandr Pushkin by Russian artist Wassilj Tropinin.

"The Land of Moscow"
by Aleksandr Pushkin
from *The Reminiscences at Tsarskoye Selo*

The land of Moscow—the land that is my native,
Where in the dawn of my best years,
I spared the hours of carelessness, attractive,
Free of unhappiness and fears.
And you had seen the foes of my great nation,
And you were burned and covered with blood!
And I did not give up my life in immolation,
My wrathful spirit just was wild!

Where is the Moscow of hundred golden domes,
The dear beauty of the native land?
Where yore was the real peer to Rome,
The ruins, miserable, lied.
Oh, how, Moscow, for us, your sight, is awful!
The buildings of landlords and kings are fully swept,
All perished in a flame. The towers are mournful,
The villas of the rich are felled.

And where the luxury was thriving,
In shady parks and gardens, in the past,
Where myrtle was fragrant, limes were shining,
There now are just coals, ash, and dust.
At charming summer nights, when silent darkness roves,
The noisy gaiety would not appear there,
The lights are vanished over lakes and groves,
All dead and silent. All unfair.

Be calm, o, Russia's banner's holder,
Look at the stranger's quickly coming end,
On their proud necks and void of labor shoulders,
The Lord's vindictive arm is laid.
Behold: they promptly run, without look at road,
In Russian snows their blood like river's flood,
They run in dark of night, felled by famine and cold,
And swords of Russians, from behind.

—Translated by Yevgeny Bonver; edited by Dmitry Karshtedt

Literature

Russian authors wrote some of the world's greatest literary masterpieces. They wrote in all literary forms, including poetry, plays, short stories, and novels. The nineteenth century is sometimes called Russia's golden age of literature. During this time, many of Russia's most famous writers emerged and wrote the greatest works in the history of Russian literature.

Poetry

Without a doubt, Aleksandr Pushkin (1799–1837) is Russia's most beloved poet. Many people regard him as the greatest Russian writer of all time and the father of modern Russian literature. Born in Moscow to an aristocratic family, Pushkin learned how to read and speak French at a young age. He spent childhood summers at his grandmother's estate, where he listened to many Russian folktales and stories of his Russian ancestors. These stories stimulated Pushkin's imagination and would later become the inspiration for some of his written works.

A photograph of writer Anton Chekhov. Chekhov was also a physician, though he wrote more than he practiced medicine.

Pushkin wrote in a variety of literary styles, including narrative poetry, lyric poetry, plays, short stories, and novels. His most famous work is a novel in verse called *Eugene Onegin*. The novel's two main characters became the subjects of later Russian literature. Another of Pushkin's major works is *Boris Gudunov*, a historical tragedy in the style of William Shakespeare. Pushkin's *The Bronze Horseman*, about Peter the Great and St. Petersburg, is considered by many to be one of the greatest poems in Russian literature.

In several of his poems, Pushkin was critical of Russian government officials. For his political poetry, Pushkin was exiled twice—first to a southern Russian province and later to his family's estate. In 1837, he took part in a duel in defense of his wife's honor. At the age of thirty-seven, Aleksandr Pushkin died as a result of wounds he received during this duel. To the Russian literary world, Pushkin's death was considered a national tragedy. Pushkin's work inspired many of Russia's well-known writers, as well as artists, composers, and choreographers. In 1937—for the 100th anniversary of Pushkin's death—the Russian city of Tsarskoye Selo was renamed Pushkin in the writer's honor.

Plays and Short Stories

Anton Chekhov and Maksim Gorky were two Russian writers best known for their plays and

VAUDEVILLE THEATRE

UNCLE VANYA

by Anton Chekhov

in a new translation by Michael Frayn

A playbill from a production of *Uncle Vanya* at the Vaudeville Theater in Strand, London. Chekhov's plays are still widely produced today.

A turn-of-the-century photograph shows Russian playwright Maksim Gorky writing at his desk. Gorky traveled abroad in the 1920s. When he returned to the Soviet Union, he was not allowed to leave the country again.

short stories. Chekhov (1860–1904) wrote about the helplessness and hopelessness of some segments of Russian society. Although his characters are generally good and decent human beings, they are unable to improve their lives. Chekhov's most famous works are the two plays *Uncle Vanya* and *The Cherry Orchard*. Gorky (1868–1936) wrote about the unending poverty of the peasants and workers in Russia's lower class. His most popular play, *The Lower Depths*, details the unhappy lives of people living in a cheap boardinghouse.

Novels

Russia was the birthplace of several internationally acclaimed novelists. Two of Russia's greatest novelists— Leo Tolstoy and Fyodor Dostoevsky —both produced important works

In 1880, a year before his death, Fyodor Dostoevsky gave this speech on the Russian poet Aleksandr Pushkin. This speech is known as the Pushkin Address. Notice the author's scribblings on the pages.

This photograph of Leo Tolstoy was taken in 1908. Besides his fictional work, Tolstoy also wrote a memoir trilogy that tells the story of his life as an aristocrat. The books are entitled *Childhood*, *Boyhood*, and *Youth*.

during the second half of the nineteenth century. Tolstoy (1828–1910) wrote *War and Peace*, an epic novel about Napoléon's 1812 invasion of Russia. It became one of the most famous novels ever written. Tolstoy's other masterpiece is *Anna Karenina*, a tragic love story that delves into many issues related to Russia's upper-class society. Dostoevsky's (1821–1881) two most well-known novels are *Crime and Punishment* and *The Brothers Karamazov*. His dramatic novels explore the inner conflicts of the main characters and the struggle between good and evil.

Of Russia's twentieth-century novelists, Boris Pasternak and Aleksandr Solzhenitsyn are among the most prominent. Pasternak (1890–1960) was one of Russia's most highly regarded poets. Outside of Russia, however, he is best known for his epic novel *Doctor Zhivago*, published in Italy in 1957. The story is about the effects of the Russian Revolution on a Russian doctor and his family. The Soviet government banned *Doctor Zhivago*, and the book wasn't published in Russia until 1988. Pasternak won the Nobel Prize for Literature in 1958, but the Soviet government pressured him into declining the award. Solzhenitsyn (1918–) served in the Soviet army during World War II and also spent eight years in a labor camp. Some of his novels, including *One Day in the Life of Ivan Denisovich*, reflect these

experiences. Solzhenitsyn received the 1970 Nobel Prize for Literature.

Music

Some of the world's most celebrated classical music can be credited to Russian composers. Most of these works were written during the nineteenth and twentieth centuries. Russian composers wrote musical masterpieces, many of which were based on old Russian folktales and songs.

Classical Music

Mikhail Glinka (1804–1857) is considered the father of modern Russian classical music. In the first half of the nineteenth century, he created a unique national sound by combining old tunes from Russia with harmonies from western Europe. Two of Glinka's works are the oldest Russian operas still performed today. During the second half of the nineteenth century, Russian composer Pyotr Tchaikovsky wrote symphonies, operas, and ballets. Many of them became world famous, including the ballets *Swan Lake*, *Sleeping Beauty*, and *The Nutcracker*. Tchaikovsky also wrote an opera based on *Eugene Onegin*, the legendary novel in verse by Aleksandr Pushkin.

Early in the twentieth century, Sergey Rachmaninoff and Igor Stravinsky dominated Russian classical music. Rachmaninoff (1873–1943) is considered one of the greatest pianists of all time. He is best known for his lyrical piano compositions. Stravinsky (1882–1971) began as a student of another famous Russian composer, Nikolay Rimsky-Korsakov. Many of Stravinsky's best-known compositions were based on Russian folktales. These include three major ballets—*The Firebird*, *Petrushka*, and *The Rite of Spring*. Both Rachmaninoff and Stravinsky left Russia around the time of the Russian Revolution.

Folk Music

Folk music is very popular in Russia. Folk musicians, often dressed in traditional costumes, play musical instruments and sing songs at fairs and festivals throughout Russia. Some musicians play the balalaika, which is a Russian stringed musical instrument. It is similar to a guitar but has a triangular body, long neck, and only three strings. Balalaika musicians generally pluck the instrument's strings with a pick as accompaniment to folk songs and dances.

Some folk singers perform *byliny*, which are poetic folk songs that are half sung and half spoken. These songs are loosely based on historical events dating from the eleventh to the sixteenth centuries. They tell colorful tales of legendary Russian folk heroes. In olden times, byliny were presented by performers who traveled from one village to the next to earn a living. Over the years, they were passed down by word of mouth. Russia's folk musicians and byliny performers breathe new life into old music and preserve the history and cultural traditions of rural Russia.

Dance

Russia has a rich tradition in the performing arts, including ballet and folk dancing. Russian ballet began in the mid-eighteenth century but didn't receive worldwide fame until the mid-nineteenth century. Russian folk dances, on the other hand, have been performed for many centuries.

Ballet

Russia is internationally renowned for its ballet companies and their prized

Young women twirl in traditional folk costumes in St. Petersburg. While the women dance, the men keep time by clapping.

Performers of the Kirov Ballet company dance in a new production of Tchaikovsky's *The Nutcracker*. The Kirov Ballet is known for its romantic and traditional style of dance. *The Nutcracker* remains one of the most popular ballets during the holiday season.

dancers. Two of the most famous ballet companies in the world are the Bolshoi Ballet in Moscow and the Kirov Ballet in St. Petersburg. The Kirov trained some of the most talented ballet dancers of the twentieth century, including Rudolf Nureyev and Mikhail Baryshnikov. Both of these star performers, however, eventually left their homeland to live in the West. They wanted to enjoy the artistic freedoms that were not allowed under the strict Soviet government.

Rudolf Nureyev (1938–1993) was born near Irkutsk in the Soviet Union. In 1958, he joined the Kirov Ballet and quickly became its leading performer. He often danced with Margot Fonteyn, a famous British ballerina. While on tour in Paris in 1961, Nureyev defected to the West. He then performed with several ballet and modern dance companies in Europe and North America. In addition to dancing, Nureyev became a well-respected choreographer and also directed the Paris Opera Ballet.

Mikhail Baryshnikov was born in 1948 in Riga, Soviet Union. At the age of twelve, he began studying ballet. By the age of nineteen, Baryshnikov had become

Mikhail Baryshnikov practices ballet in his studio. Among his many awards, Baryshnikov received an Oscar nomination in 1977 for his role in the movie *Turning Point*.

a solo performer with the Kirov Ballet. In 1974, he defected to Canada and soon afterward joined the American Ballet Theatre in New York City. He went on to perform with the New York City Ballet and later became artistic director of the American Ballet Theatre. Baryshnikov has also appeared in several films.

Folk Dancing

In Russia, folk dancing has remained popular over the centuries. Folk dancers perform at a variety of festive occasions, including weddings, festivals, and country fairs. They often wear traditional costumes made of brightly colored cloth and featuring intricate embroidery work. Many of Russia's ethnic groups perform their own unique dances for special events and celebrations. Some of these folk dances relate stories of Russian life, culture, and tradition. Others are designed to celebrate certain times of the year, such as the beginning of spring or harvesttime.

Koryak dancers perform in their traditional costumes. Koryaks are one of Russia's many ethnic groups. They inhabit coastal areas near the Bering Sea.

FAMOUS FOODS AND RECIPES OF RUSSIA

9

Throughout the world, Russians are well known for their great hospitality. They love food and enjoy sharing a hearty meal with family and friends. Even unexpected guests are welcomed to the table, and no one leaves hungry. Russian people have a tradition of greeting visitors with an offering of bread and salt. One of the Russian words for hospitality is *khlebosol'stvo*, which comes from the Russian words for bread *(khleb)* and salt *(sol)*.

Everyday Food

In Russia, most families live in apartments or small houses. Kitchens are usually not very large, and refrigerator and cabinet space is limited. In addition, people who live in the city often use public transportation rather than own their own cars. For these reasons, many Russians shop for food every day. That way, they don't have to carry a lot of grocery bags on the train or subway or find storage space for large quantities of food.

Although most cities in Russia have large supermarkets, many Russians shop at local farmers'

At left, women sell melons and squash at a vegetable market in Moscow. Squash is a staple side dish to a traditional Russian meal. Above, a man ice fishes on Lake Baikal in Siberia. Lake Baikal has one of the most diverse populations of fish of any freshwater body of water in the world. It is a popular place to fish in all weather.

A hot bowl of borscht is good medicine for a cold, wintry day. Its name comes from the Russian word *borshch*, which means cow parsnip, a vegetable from which the soup was originally made.

markets. There, they can choose from a colorful array of fruits, vegetables, and baked goods. Because of the long winters, however, fresh foods may not always be available. Some crops don't grow well in Russia's cold climate and must be imported from other areas. Russian cooks are experts at making the most of the resources they have available. Soups and stews, for example, provide warm and hearty meals that can be made with an assortment of on-hand ingredients. Borscht is a popular Russian soup made with beets and a variety of other vegetables.

Some traditional Russian dishes, including borscht, are part of a cooking heritage passed down from the Russian peasants before the revolution. Other dishes, such as beef Stroganoff, came from the meals enjoyed by the Russian nobility of pre-revolution times.

In Russia, the largest meal of the day is dinner, which is usually served between 12:00 and 2:00 in the afternoon. A traditional dinner typically includes three or four courses and starts with *zakuski,* or appetizers. Although "zakuski" is Russian for "little bites," it's actually quite substantial fare. Zakuski might include caviar, smoked fish, cold meats, and cheeses. The next course is usually a soup, such as borscht. Then comes the main course, which generally consists of beef, chicken, or fish, along with potatoes, rice, or noodles. Bread is very popular in Russia and is usually served with every meal. Dinner often concludes with hot tea served from a samovar, and pastries or other dessert foods.

Blini

Ingredients

4 C. flour   1 tbsp. sugar
2 C. buttermilk   1 tsp. salt
1 egg   Assorted toppings

Preparation

Put flour in a large mixing bowl. Add buttermilk
   slowly, stirring well.

Add egg, sugar, and salt to the flour mixture,
   stirring until well blended. The mixture should
   look like pancake batter. If it's too thick, add small amounts of warm water
   until the right consistency is reached. Allow batter to stand and thicken for
   about 10 minutes.

Lightly coat the bottom of a small skillet with a small amount (about 1 teaspoon)
   of vegetable oil. Heat skillet over medium heat.

Pour about ¼ cup batter into the heated skillet, tilting the pan so that the
   batter covers the bottom.

After two minutes or so, use a spatula to lift the edge of the blini. When the
   bottom of the blini is light brown, flip it over.

When the bottom of the other side is light brown, remove blini from the skillet
   and put it on a plate. Cover the blini with a cloth towel to keep warm and moist.

Repeat this process to make additional blini with the remaining batter. More oil
   can be added to the skillet as needed.

Serve blini warm and topped with butter, sour cream, jam, or fresh fruit, such
   as blueberries or sliced strawberries.

Makes 4 to 6 servings.

Source: *Cooking the Russian Way*, by Gregory and Rita Plotkin

Food for Special Occasions

As in many cultures, holidays and festivals are cause for celebration in Russia. These special occasions include Russian Orthodox holidays, such as Easter and Christmas. They also include secular holidays, such as New Year's Day, and seasonal and harvest festivals. Russians consider these occasions to be the perfect time to gather together with family and friends and celebrate with special meals.

Because Easter is the most important holiday in the Russian Orthodox Church, it merits the biggest celebrations. Most Russian Orthodox Christians fast for Lent in the weeks preceding Easter Sunday. During Lent, they don't eat meat or dairy products. Just before Lent begins, Russians celebrate with lots of food and festivities during Butter Week. A traditional favorite food at this time of year is blini—thin pancakes served with butter, sour cream, and other toppings.

After Lent is over and the fasting has ended, Russians celebrate Easter. Food for the Easter feast is prepared during the entire week leading up to the holiday. The main course might be ham, veal, or roast lamb. A special treat served at most Easter dinners is *kulich*—sweet bread made with raisins and nuts and topped

The first McDonald's restaurant opened in Moscow's Puskin Square on January 31, 1990. The Pushkin Square McDonald's is the largest in the world. It seats 700 and has 27 cash registers.

with icing. Kulich is baked in a shape that resembles the tall hat worn by Russian Orthodox priests. Painted Easter eggs are another traditional holiday favorite. At midnight on the eve of Easter, Russian Orthodox Christians attend church services. Many bring the food they have prepared for Easter so that the priest can bless it. When they arrive home from church, the feast begins.

In Russia, New Year's celebrations often incorporate many Russian Orthodox Christmas traditions. Starting in the Soviet era and continuing to this day, the festivities for New Year's Day are often grander than those for Christmas. There are gifts and sweets for the children and parties for the adults. The highlight of the day is a festive holiday meal for the whole family.

A woman inspects and bottles vodka at the Stolichnaya factory in Mariinsk. Stolichnaya is one of the finest brands of Russian vodka. It is exported all over the world.

DAILY LIFE AND CUSTOMS IN RUSSIA

10

Since the end of Soviet rule, life in Russia has changed considerably. In some ways, daily life in Russia today is similar to daily life in the United States. For example, many Russians enjoy the same sports and leisure activities that Americans do. In other ways, daily life in Russia is very different. For instance, it is rare for a family to own a home, and many families don't own a car.

Living Conditions

The majority of people in Russia live in large towns or cities. Russian cities are very over-crowded. That doesn't stop people from moving into them, however, to find work. Many Russians also enjoy taking part in the activities of city life, such as visiting a museum, spending an evening at the theater, or attending the ballet or opera.

Most Russians who live in the city have small apartments in large high-rise apartment buildings. These buildings were constructed during the Soviet era. Each apartment typically has

At left is the gigantic GUM store in Moscow. The mall was built in 1900 and is located in Red Square. It has over 1,000 shops and is the most popular shopping destination in Moscow. Above is an aerial view of a block of apartment high-rises in a modern neighborhood in St. Petersburg near the Gulf of Finland.

A highly decorated Russian country house, or *dacha*. Dachas can become very secluded during the winter. High snowdrifts in the countryside block roads and prevent anyone from leaving or coming to these houses. Because of these conditions, most vacationers use their dachas during the summer.

one or two small bedrooms, a living room, an eat-in kitchen, and one bathroom. The living room often doubles as an additional bedroom in the evenings. In many apartments, large extended families live together, creating a very crowded space.

Some lucky city dwellers own a dacha—a small wooden cottage in the country—where they can go to relax on weekends during the summer. Some dachas have electricity but lack other conveniences, such as running water. Many families keep a garden at their dacha, where they grow their own vegetables.

For those Russians who don't live in cities or towns, home is in the country. People who live in rural areas usually work on farms, tending the crops and animals. Although country life is slower and more relaxed than city life, it has its share of hardships. Most homes have electricity, but some lack indoor plumbing. Villages are often located far away from one another, and transportation is difficult because there are few paved

A grandmother gardens outside while her granddaughter peers through the window of their dacha. Russian children often have close, special bonds with their grandparents.

roads. Schools and health facilities in the country have limited supplies.

Family Life

Family is very important in Russia, and family life revolves around the children. Many Russian parents make huge sacrifices to provide for their children, giving them the best possible home, food, and clothing. In addition, they often spoil the children by giving them any special treats or luxuries they can afford.

In Russian families, it's fairly common for the grandmother to live in the home. Known as the *babushka*, the grandmother often moves in with the family after her husband passes away. In many Russian homes, both parents must work to support the family. A live-in babushka helps out by caring for the young children while the parents are at work. Many babushkas also take care of the household chores, including grocery shopping, cooking, and cleaning.

Team Sports

In Russia, sports are a popular pastime. The national sport of Russia, as well as many countries of the former Soviet Union, is ice hockey. Russia has produced some

Young girls visit the ice rink to cheer their favorite hockey players. Many young children in Russia dream of becoming famous professional hockey players.

of the best ice hockey players of all time. Since the collapse of the Soviet Union, many Russian hockey players now play for the National Hockey League (NHL) in North America.

As in many countries, the most popular sport in Russia is soccer. Crowds fill the stands at professional soccer matches throughout Russia, and fans are devoted to their favorite team. Started in Europe—and known there as football—soccer was introduced to Russia in the late 1800s and quickly grew in popularity. Team sports, including soccer, were promoted and sponsored by the Communist government during the Soviet period. Today, many of Russia's best players have moved to western Europe or North America to play in professional soccer leagues.

Two American team sports that have gained popularity in Russia are basketball and volleyball. Because of Russia's harsh climate, many outdoor sports can't be played during much of the year. Basketball and volleyball are good choices because they can be played on indoor courts. Russia has both men's and women's basketball and volleyball teams.

Olympic Sports

Every four years, athletes from around the world come together to participate in the Olympic Games. At this international sports event, athletes compete for gold, silver, and bronze medals in a wide array of individual and team sports. Summer sports range from track and field events to swimming and diving competitions. Winter sports include skiing, bobsledding, and speed skating. For many years, the Summer and Winter Olympics were held in the same year. More recently, Winter and Summer Olympic Games have alternated every two years.

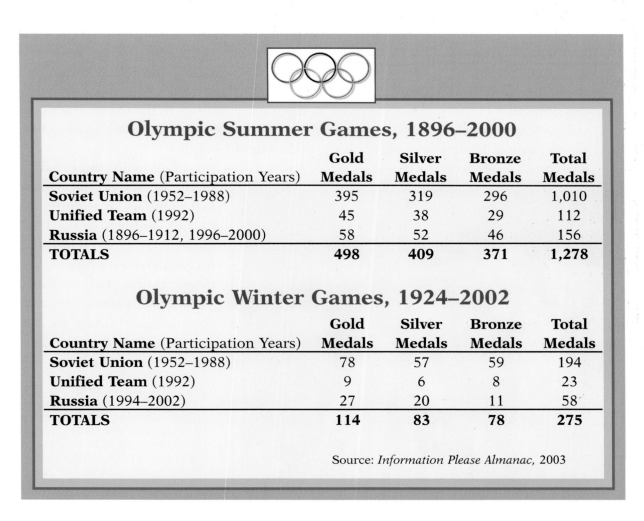

Olympic Summer Games, 1896–2000

Country Name (Participation Years)	Gold Medals	Silver Medals	Bronze Medals	Total Medals
Soviet Union (1952–1988)	395	319	296	1,010
Unified Team (1992)	45	38	29	112
Russia (1896–1912, 1996–2000)	58	52	46	156
TOTALS	498	409	371	1,278

Olympic Winter Games, 1924–2002

Country Name (Participation Years)	Gold Medals	Silver Medals	Bronze Medals	Total Medals
Soviet Union (1952–1988)	78	57	59	194
Unified Team (1992)	9	6	8	23
Russia (1994–2002)	27	20	11	58
TOTALS	114	83	78	275

Source: *Information Please Almanac*, 2003

In 2002, Irina Slutskaya competed in the Hallmark Skater's Championship in Columbus, Ohio. Slutskaya went on that year to become an Olympic silver medalist.

Russia has always been a dominant force at both the Summer and Winter Olympics, especially during the Soviet era. During the Cold War years, the Olympic Games set the stage for the bitter rivalry between the Communist-led Soviet Union and the democratic United States. Determined to win the battle, the USSR made sure that its competitors were some of the most highly trained athletes in the world. For many years, Soviet athletes excelled in numerous Olympic events, including gymnastics, figure skating, ice hockey, pole vaulting, and weightlifting.

Following the breakup of the Soviet Union, Russia lost some of its dominance at the Olympics. At the 1992 games, athletes from the former Soviet countries competed as the Unified Team. The USSR separation became complete, however, at the

World chess champion Vladimir Kramnik concentrates on his next move at the Sparkassen Chess Meeting in Dortmund, Germany, in 2003. Kramnik is one of the world's top chess players. He left the 2003 Sparkassen Chess Meeting unbeaten.

An ice swimmer climbs out of a lake after a refreshing swim in Moscow Park. Ice swimming is usually done in the morning when the weather is the coldest. Many Russians believe that ice swimming improves circulation and general health.

1994 Winter Olympics. During that contest, the nations of the former Soviet Union began competing as independent countries. Although Russia hasn't kept the supremacy held by the Soviet Union, it has amassed one of the best Olympic medal records of any country in history.

Games and Pastimes

Entertainment is a vital part of daily life in Russia. Both children and adults enjoy playing games and taking part in outdoor activities. A favorite game of many Russians, young and old, is chess. Chess is so popular, in fact, that Russians play it everywhere—in restaurants, hotel lobbies, trains, and public parks. National chess tournaments have millions of participants. Some Russian schools even teach chess as part of the standard curriculum. In addition to chess, backgammon, dominoes, and card games are also popular in Russia.

Many favorite Russian pastimes revolve around the country's cold climate and long winters. Most Russian children, for example, enjoy ice-skating on frozen lakes or sledding down snow-covered hills. Some Russians take the cold-weather fun a step further by going swimming in icy water. These swimmers, known as "walruses" or "polar bears," feel that a midwinter swim in a nearly frozen lake is a refreshing treat!

EDUCATION AND WORK IN RUSSIA

11

During the time of the Soviet Union, the Communist government wanted the country to become an industrial superpower. For this goal to be achieved, Soviet workers needed to be well educated and well trained. So the Soviet government started a new program in which education was free and all children were required to attend school. Although the Soviet education system had several benefits, it also had drawbacks. Students learned by memorization and were discouraged from critical thinking or analysis. Children were taught about the many benefits of Communism and the many ills of democracy. Soviet textbooks reinvented history to make the Soviet Union look like the winner in every world event.

In the workplace, there were similar advantages and disadvantages during the Soviet era. On the positive side, unemployment was almost nonexistent. Everyone had a job. On the negative side, the government owned all of the farms and factories where people worked. The government set workers' wages, which were very low. Workers were not rewarded with more money for working harder. Under the Communist system, owning a private business was illegal.

Since the breakup of the Soviet Union, Russia's educational system has undergone many changes. Education is still very important in modern Russia. Now,

At left, a young girl studies at her desk. Above, Russian children don't bring apples to impress their teachers, they bring flowers. The first day of school is cause for celebration in Russia. After a long summer of playing, many children are anxious to come back to school and see their friends and teachers again.

however, students are being encouraged to ask questions, use their imaginations, and think for themselves. They are taught about other cultures and the world around them, not just about Russia. Over time, as schools can afford them, factual history textbooks are replacing inaccurate Soviet-era books.

In the world of work, many changes have also taken place since the fall of Communism. But change has come slowly and not without problems. The old Communist system has been converted to a free-market economy. Government-owned farms and factories have been transferred over to businesses and private owners. Many workplaces have needed to be modernized, however, and the new owners often can't afford new equipment. Some businesses, unable to earn a profit, have had to close their doors. One positive change in Russia's workplace has been the growth of small privately owned businesses.

Education

Before 1917, the illiteracy rate in Russia was very high. More than 75 percent of the Russian population didn't know how to read or write. After the Soviet rulers took control of the government, they made a ten-year education compulsory. Between the ages of seven and seventeen, all Russian children had to attend school. This government-mandated education created a huge increase in Russia's literacy rate. Today, 98 percent of all Russian citizens can read and write.

The Russian school year begins on September 1 and continues through the end of June. Summer vacation takes place in July and August. Traditionally, students bring a flower for their teacher on the first day of school. Many Russian children attend school six days a week, with Sunday as their only day off. Classes start between 8:00 and 8:30 in the morning. While classes end at 12:30 PM for young children, the school day continues until 2:30 PM for older children.

Some young children go to preschool and kindergarten, but school is not a requirement until children are six or seven years old. After completing ninth grade, students can choose whether or not they want to continue their education. Some attend a regular high school, while others go to a vocational high school to learn a specialized skill or trade. After high school, some students continue on to earn a college degree at a university.

At left is a Communist propaganda poster from 1920. The poster reads "On the ruins of capitalism, let us walk towards brotherhood! Peasants, workers, let us walk towards the people of the world!" Posters like these were everywhere in Russia after the Bolshevik Revolution.

A line of cadets marches through the town of Derbent in the Republic of Daghestan. Cadet school is a military college for young Russians. Many cadets go on to serve in the Russian army after graduation.

Primary and Middle School

Beginning at age six or seven, children in Russia attend primary school for grades one through four. Then they move on to middle school for grades five through nine. Russian students are taught reading, writing, mathematics, science, social studies, and a foreign language, such as English. As early as first grade, Russian students learn complex math and science.

Each night, students often must complete one to two hours of homework assignments. Russian students are graded on a scale of one to five, with five being the highest grade. After classes each day, many students stay at school to take part in after-school sports, such as soccer.

Secondary School

After finishing middle school, students in Russia take a national exam. Those students who do well on the exam may elect to attend secondary school, or high school. In high school, students

The State University in Moscow was founded by Mikhail Lomonosov, an eighteenth-century Russian scholar and scientist. The university opened its library in 1756. For over 100 years it was the only library in Moscow.

focus on one specific course of study, such as mathematics, science, social studies, literature, or sports. Those students who received low scores on the national exam may choose to attend a vocational high school, or trade school. There, they will learn a trade, such as medical technology or auto mechanics.

University

Only about 25 percent of Russian students continue their education after high school. To be admitted to a university or other institution of higher learning, they must perform very well on a difficult entrance exam. Earning a college-level degree at a Russian university takes five years. Some of the graduates from Russian universities try to immigrate to Europe or North America to live and work.

Russia has several hundred institutes of higher education. With about 40,000 students, Moscow University is Russia's largest university. Founded in 1755, it's also the oldest and most well-known university in the country.

The Russian Economy

Before 1917, Russia was a relatively undeveloped country with few industries. Most people worked on farms, rather than in factories. Russia did not produce many goods or services for trade in the world market. Shortly after the Communist takeover, the country's economy did a major turnaround, becoming one of the most powerful in the world. The reason was that the Communist government owned all of the nation's natural resources and industries. The government made all the decisions about the industries to be developed, production quotas to be met, prices for goods, and wages paid to workers.

This Communist system worked well for the government for a while, but not so well for the workers. Under Communist

Russian peasants harvest carrots. Many Russians living in the countryside who cannot afford to maintain their own farms work as migrant farmers.

A large oil pipeline is repaired by the Yukos Oil Company. Oil, natural gas, timber, and metal account for 80 percent of Russia's exports.

rule, the Soviet Union became an industrialized nation. But this progress came at a high cost. The people lost their individual freedoms, and their standard of living declined. Since the fall of Communism, the Russian people have regained many of their individual rights and freedoms. Slowly, Russia's free-market economy has also been improving.

The World of Work

Russia is a vast land that is rich in natural resources. These resources include fertile farmlands; immense forests; large supplies of energy sources, such as coal, oil, and natural gas; and enormous deposits of minerals, such as copper, nickel, iron, and gold. Many of these natural resources, though, are found in the far reaches of Siberia. The region's harsh climate and limited transportation often make access very difficult. Still, many people in Russia work in industries related to these natural resources.

Working the Land

Only about 10 percent of the land in Russia is suitable for agriculture. However, the fertile farmland that does exist enables Russia to be one of the world's leading producers of grains. These grains, including wheat and barley, are grown chiefly in the steppe region and do well in Russia's short, dry summer climate. Other crops grown in Russia include fruits, such as melons and cherries, and vegetables, such as potatoes, beets, and peppers. Russian farmland is also good for raising livestock, including cattle, goats, pigs, and chickens. Some types of livestock are

North Korean lumberjacks work in Russia for cheap wages. In return for lending cheap labor to Russia, North Korea receives a portion of Russia's timber.

raised to produce milk and eggs, while other types are raised for food. About 13 percent of the people in Russia work in agriculture.

Russia's extensive waterways, including lakes, rivers, and oceans, help to make fishing an important industry. Large fishing fleets catch a variety of seafood in Russian waters, including salmon, herring, haddock, and cod. The most well-known Russian seafood is caviar, which is an expensive luxury food made of roe (fish eggs) from sturgeon. Problems with pollution and overfishing have led to smaller catches in Russia in recent years.

The Russian landscape contains more than 20 percent of the world's forests, including nearly half of the world's coniferous forests. Coniferous trees are evergreen trees that bear cones, such as pine trees. Most of Russia's forests are located in Asian Russia. Although Russian logging companies do work in these forests, access to them is difficult. Consequently, Russia has sold many timbering rights to companies located in eastern Asia, from which access to the forests is easier.

Mining and Manufacturing

Some of the world's largest supplies of energy sources are located in Russia. Western Siberia and the Ural Mountains boast some of the largest oil reserves in the world. As much as 35 percent of the world's natural gas supply can be found in Russia. The country supplies much of western Europe's natural gas. Another of Russia's plentiful energy resources is coal. In the twenty-first century, Russia is self-reliant in terms of energy production and use. It is also a leading producer of the world's energy supply, exporting more than 35 percent of all oil and natural gas extracted.

Aerial view of a diamond mine in Jakutia. The Grib Pipe is a site that was discovered in 1996 in Siberia. It is the largest deposit of diamonds outside of South Africa.

In addition to energy sources, nearly every major mineral can be found in Russia. The world's largest iron ore reserves are found in Russia, with significant deposits in the Ural Mountains and in southwestern Siberia. Russia is the world's second-largest producer of nickel, which is mined in the Kola Peninsula and in the southern Urals. Copper and bauxite are also plentiful minerals. Russia is one of the world's largest producers of gold, which is mined in Siberia. Large quantities of diamonds are also mined in Siberia.

Russia's vast array of natural resources helps to make manufacturing an essential part of the country's economy. Many manufacturing plants and factories are located in the cities of Moscow and St. Petersburg. Workers in manufacturing plants take raw materials such as timber, oil, and iron ore and convert them into such products as lumber, petroleum, and steel. In factories, these products are then used to build cars, machinery, and other equipment. Today, more Russian factories are producing consumer products, including furniture, clothing, and household appliances.

On a park bench in Moscow, a homeless man takes a nap. Struggling in a post-Communist economy, many Russians have difficulty finding jobs and affording a place to live. There are an estimated 300,000 homeless people living in Moscow.

The Future of Russia

In the post-Soviet era, many challenges lie ahead for Russia. The conversion from a Communist economy to a free-market economy has been a slow and difficult process. State-owned factories and businesses were sold to private companies, but many new owners lacked the resources to replace outdated and inefficient equipment. Many people lost their jobs when these businesses shut down. Farmers who worked on government-owned farms often couldn't afford to buy the land or the equipment they needed to make it on their own. During the 1990s, rates of unemployment and inflation rose significantly.

In the early twenty-first century, however, Russia's economy began to rebound. Rates of unemployment and inflation have fallen steadily, and income levels are on the rise. Consumer goods have become more available and more affordable. With the new right to own their own businesses, some Russian entrepreneurs have opened small restaurants, clothing shops, and hair salons. However, the change to privately owned businesses has caused a growing gap between the rich and the poor in Russia. Although Russia's future remains uncertain, there is definitely cause for optimism.

RUSSIA
AT A GLANCE

HISTORY

Russia was first settled in the sixth century by Slavs. During the ninth century, Vikings gained control of the Slavic lands and founded a new state called Kievan Rus. Kiev became the capital of Kievan Rus, and Prince Vladimir was its ruler. In 988, Prince Vladimir made Christianity the state religion, with most of his subjects practicing Eastern Orthodoxy.

By the thirteenth century, civil wars had weakened the power of Kievan Rus, leaving it vulnerable to an invasion by Mongol armies. Following the invasion, Russia became part of the Mongol Empire in an area called the Golden Horde. Nearly 250 years later, the Mongol occupation finally ended when Ivan the Great and his armies drove the invaders out of Russia.

In the seventeenth century, the Romanov family began a three-hundred-year dynasty as rulers of Russia. The Romanov dynasty was a time of serfdom when most Russian people lived in near slavery. By the turn of the twentieth century, the Russian people had grown extremely unhappy with the czars' rule. During a peaceful march in 1905, hundreds of Russian workers were killed or injured when government soldiers opened fired on the crowd of protesters.

In the early twentieth century, Russia fought against Austria-Hungary and Germany in World War I. The war effort caused severe food and fuel shortages for the Russian people, and in 1917, they rioted over these shortages. By that time, Czar Nicholas II had lost his political power and was forced to abdicate the throne. The Bolshevik Party, led by V. I. Lenin, planned a revolt that overthrew the Russian government.

Following this revolt, Communist (formerly known as Bolshevik) forces fought in a civil war against anti-Communist forces for control of Russia. The Communists won, and Lenin became the country's new leader. Lenin established new policies in which the government controlled Russia's economy. Russia joined with other territories to form a new country called the Union of Soviet Socialist Republics (USSR), or the Soviet Union. After Lenin died in 1924, Joseph Stalin took control as the leader of both the Communist Party and the Soviet Union. People who spoke out against Stalin's policies were sent to prison labor camps or executed.

During World War II, the Soviet Union began fighting on the side of Germany. After Germany invaded the country, however, the Soviet Union switched sides and began fighting against Germany. During the Battle of Stalingrad, Soviet troops drove the German armies out of the country. Soviet forces went on to capture Berlin, helping to end World War II. After the war, tensions mounted between the Soviet Union and the United States, beginning a long and intense rivalry known as the Cold War.

Following Joseph Stalin's death in 1953, Nikita Khrushchev became the new leader of the Soviet Union. During his rule, some restrictions imposed by the Soviet government were eased. By the time Mikhail Gorbachev took over as Soviet leader in 1985, however, the Soviet people were ready for change. Gorbachev introduced several new policies, including perestroika (economic restructuring) and glasnost (openness). Although he tried to reform the country's economy, his new policies ultimately failed. After Gorbachev resigned at the end of 1991, the Soviet Union was formally dissolved.

Boris Yeltsin became the first Russian leader to be elected by the people. Under his leadership, Russia began the difficult shift to a free-market economy. Yeltsin resigned at the end of 1999. In 2000, Vladimir Putin was elected president of Russia.

ECONOMY

For most of the twentieth century, the Russian economy as well as that of the rest of the Soviet Union was based on Communism. With this system, the government owned and controlled all land, property, and businesses. It also maintained control over nearly all aspects of production. The Communist Party dominated all areas of economic activity in the Soviet Union.

Following the collapse of the Soviet Union and the fall of Communism in 1991, the Russian economy entered a period of decline. The resulting shortages of consumer goods led to long lines at stores. To resolve this situation, the new Russian government began the conversion to a free-market economy, where businesses set their own prices.

For the last decade of the twentieth century, this transition proved to be quite challenging for Russia. No longer controlled by the state, the economy now operated on the basis of market forces. Russians were inexperienced with this type of economy, and many problems arose. Outdated technology and equipment also made it difficult for Russian industry to keep pace with the rest of the world.

By the early part of the twenty-first century, the Russian economy had begun to rebound. In 2002, Russia's gross domestic product (GDP) increased by more than 4 percent. This rate of growth exceeded that of the United States, France, Britain, Italy, Germany, Canada, and Japan.

Although the economy has improved, many Russian citizens still struggle to make ends meet. According to official government estimates, nearly 25 percent of Russia's population has an income level that is below the poverty line. Other sources, however, indicate that the number of Russian citizens living in poverty is actually closer to 50 percent of the population. Despite these statistics, a small number of Russians are extremely wealthy. In 2002, ten of Russia's richest citizens appeared on *Forbes* magazine's list of billionaires. In 2003, the number of Russian billionaires on the list had increased to seventeen.

Even though it's only half as large as the former Soviet economy, the Russian economy includes a wealth of resources. Russia's landscape contains an abundant supply of many of the world's most prized natural resources, including oil, natural gas, coal, platinum, gold, silver, diamonds, and other precious gemstones. Vast supplies of timber, uranium, nickel, iron ore, phosphates, potash, sodium chloride, cobalt, titanium, tungsten, copper, lead, zinc, bauxite, tin, magnesium, and mercury are also found in Russia.

In addition to mining or extracting coal, oil, gas, chemicals, and metals, Russian industry produces all types of machines. Russian industry also supplies transportation and communications equipment; agricultural machinery, tractors, and construction equipment; electric power–generating and –transmitting equipment; medical and scientific instruments; and consumer goods, textiles, foodstuffs, and handicrafts.

Russia is the largest exporter of natural gas in the world, as well as the second-largest exporter of oil (following Saudi Arabia). Other major Russian exports include wood and wood products, metals, chemicals, and a wide variety of civilian and military manufactures. Russia's major imports include machinery and equipment, consumer goods, medicines, meat, sugar, and semifinished metal products.

GOVERNMENT AND POLITICS

Today, Russia is a federation, with executive, legislative, and judicial branches of government. Its capital city is Moscow. Russia has both a president, who is the chief of state, and a prime minister, who is the head of government. Currently, Russia's president is Vladimir Putin, who was first elected to office in 2000. The president, who is the country's most powerful official, serves a four-year term and can be reelected. Russia's current prime minister is Mikhail Kasyanov. The ministries of the government are composed of the premier and his deputies, ministers, and selected other individuals. The president appoints all cabinet members.

Russia's parliament is called the Federal Assembly. It consists of two houses—the State Duma, with 450 members, and the Federation Council, with 178 members. The State Duma is responsible for creating Russia's laws. Proposed legislation does not become law, however, until both the Federation Council and the president approve it. The Federation Council is responsible for approving government appointments and certain actions ordered by the president.

Before March 1990, the Communist Party was the only legal political party in the Soviet Union. The Soviet Constitution had given the Communist Party a great amount of power. After the collapse of the Soviet Union, however, the country's constitution was amended. Today, Russia has a large number of political parties.

Although the Communist Party remains a powerful force in the State Duma, other political parties are also well represented. These parties include Russia's Democratic Choice, the Liberal Democratic Party, Our Home Is Russia, Unity, Fatherland—All Russia, the Union of Right Wing Forces, and Yabloko.

Russia's legal system is based on a civil law system, which includes judicial review of legislative acts. The civil rights of all Russian citizens are protected under Russia's 1993 Constitution. Established in 1992, the Constitutional Court is Russia's highest court. It provides rulings on whether Russia's laws are constitutional.

Since 1994, the Russian military has been involved in a dispute over the independence of Chechnya. Chechnya is a Russian republic located in the Caucasus Mountains along Russia's southwestern border. Thousands of Chechens have been killed in the conflict, and thousands of others have fled their homeland because of the fighting.

TIMELINE

500
Early Slavs travel from central Asia and settle in European Russia.

988
Prince Vladimir, the ruler of Kiev, converts to Christianity. He makes Christianity the state religion, and most of his subjects convert.

1237
Mongol armies, led by Batu Khan, invade Russia from central Asia.

1480
Mongol rule finally ends when Prince Ivan III ousts the invaders and declares himself czar of Russia.

800
A Viking tribe gains control of the Slavic lands and founds a new state called Kievan Rus. Kiev becomes the capital.

1240
Mongol invaders destroy Kiev, and Kievan Rus falls. Russia is integrated into the Mongol Empire within the Golden Horde.

1894
Nicholas II becomes Russia's last czar.

1914
World War I begins. Russia, France, and Great Britain join forces to fight against Austria-Hungary and Germany.

1918
After more than a year in captivity, Czar Nicholas II, his wife, and his family are executed.

1905
Hundreds of peaceful Russian protesters are injured or killed when government soldiers open fire on them. The event becomes known as Bloody Sunday.

1917
The Bolsheviks lead a revolution to oust Czar Nicholas II from power and take over the government. V. I. Lenin becomes the first leader of the Soviet Union.

1924
Lenin dies, and Joseph Stalin takes over as leader of the Communist Party.

1963
Soviet cosmonaut Valentina Tereshkova becomes the first woman to orbit the Earth.

1964
Khrushchev is overthrown, and Leonid Brezhnev takes over as leader of the USSR.

1979
The Soviet Union invades Afghanistan.

1989
The Cold War ends, and Germany's Berlin Wall is torn down.

1985
Mikhail Gorbachev becomes general secretary of the Soviet Union.

1990
Russia declares independence from the USSR.

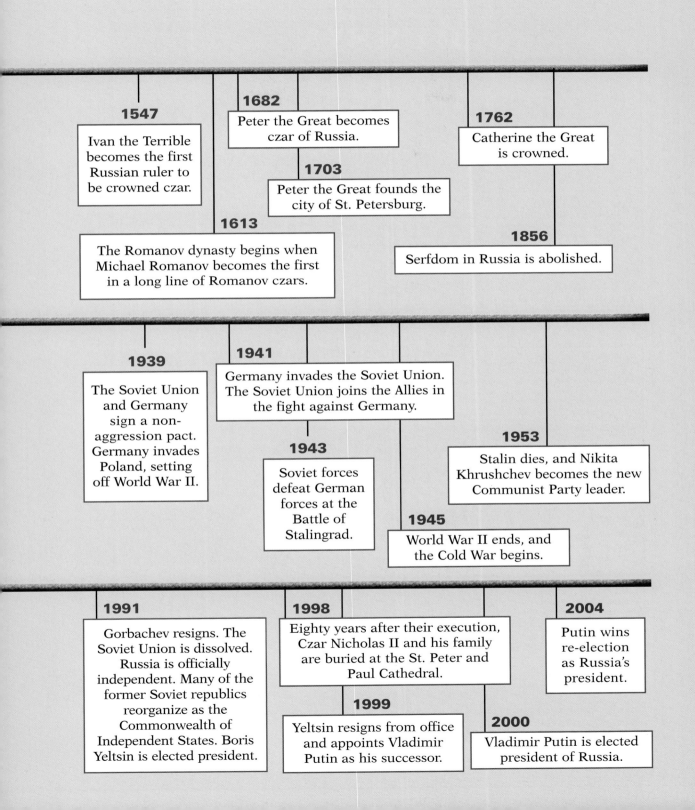

1547
Ivan the Terrible becomes the first Russian ruler to be crowned czar.

1682
Peter the Great becomes czar of Russia.

1703
Peter the Great founds the city of St. Petersburg.

1762
Catherine the Great is crowned.

1613
The Romanov dynasty begins when Michael Romanov becomes the first in a long line of Romanov czars.

1856
Serfdom in Russia is abolished.

1939
The Soviet Union and Germany sign a non-aggression pact. Germany invades Poland, setting off World War II.

1941
Germany invades the Soviet Union. The Soviet Union joins the Allies in the fight against Germany.

1943
Soviet forces defeat German forces at the Battle of Stalingrad.

1945
World War II ends, and the Cold War begins.

1953
Stalin dies, and Nikita Khrushchev becomes the new Communist Party leader.

1991
Gorbachev resigns. The Soviet Union is dissolved. Russia is officially independent. Many of the former Soviet republics reorganize as the Commonwealth of Independent States. Boris Yeltsin is elected president.

1998
Eighty years after their execution, Czar Nicholas II and his family are buried at the St. Peter and Paul Cathedral.

1999
Yeltsin resigns from office and appoints Vladimir Putin as his successor.

2004
Putin wins re-election as Russia's president.

2000
Vladimir Putin is elected president of Russia.

RUSSIA

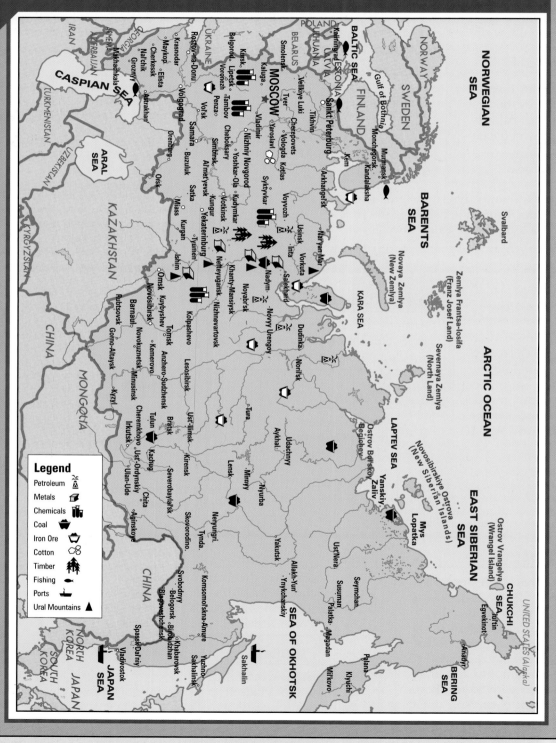

Legend
- Petroleum
- Metals
- Chemicals
- Coal
- Iron Ore
- Cotton
- Timber
- Fishing
- Ports
- Ural Mountains ▲

ECONOMIC FACT SHEET

GDP in US$: $1.35 trillion; per capita: $9,300

GDP Sectors: Agriculture 6%, industry 34.5%, services 59.5%

Currency: 1 ruble = 100 kopeks; 31.27 rubles to the US dollar

Workforce: 72 million

Workforce by Occupation: Agriculture 12%, industry 23%, services 65%

Major Agricultural Products: Wheat, rye, barley, oats, sugar beets, potatoes, rice, sunflower seed, vegetables, fruits, beef, sheep, pigs, and milk

Major Exports: Petroleum and petroleum products, natural gas, wood and wood products, metals, chemicals, and a wide variety of civilian and military products

Major Imports: Machinery and equipment, consumer goods, medicines, meat, sugar, semifinished metal products

National Resources: Oil, natural gas, coal, uranium, timber, nickel, iron ore, phosphates, potash, sodium chloride, cobalt, titanium, tungsten, copper, lead, zinc, bauxite, tin, magnesium, mercury, platinum, gold, silver, diamonds, emeralds, and many others

Significant Trading Partners:

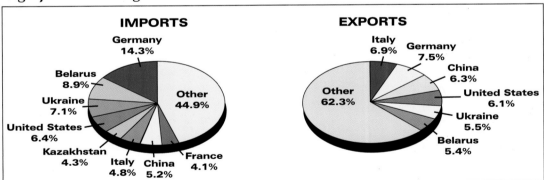

IMPORTS

- Germany 14.3%
- Belarus 8.9%
- Ukraine 7.1%
- United States 6.4%
- Kazakhstan 4.3%
- Italy 4.8%
- China 5.2%
- France 4.1%
- Other 44.9%

EXPORTS

- Italy 6.9%
- Germany 7.5%
- China 6.3%
- United States 6.1%
- Ukraine 5.5%
- Belarus 5.4%
- Other 62.3%

Rate of Unemployment: 8%

Population Below Poverty Line: 25%

Industry: Complete range of mining and extractive industries producing coal, oil, gas, chemicals, and metals; all forms of machines, from rolling mills to high-performance aircraft and space vehicles; shipbuilding; road and rail transportation equipment; communications equipment; agricultural machinery, tractors, and construction equipment; electric power generating and transmitting equipment; medical and scientific instruments; consumer goods, textiles, foodstuffs, handicrafts

POLITICAL FACT SHEET

Official Country Name:
Russian Federation
Capital: Moscow
System of Government:
Federation
Chief of State: President
Head of Government:
Prime minister
Cabinet: Ministries of the
government composed of
the premier and his
deputies, ministers, and
selected other individuals;
all appointed by the president
Legislature: Russia's parliament, called the Federal Assembly, consists of two
houses—the State Duma (450 members) and the Federation Council (178 members)
Political Subdivisions: Forty-nine oblasts (regions), twenty-one republics, ten
autonomous okrugs (areas), six krays (territories), two federal cities, and one
autonomous oblast
Independence: August 21, 1991 (from Soviet Union)
Constitution: December 12, 1993
Legal System: Based on civil law system; judicial review of legislative acts
Suffrage: Eighteen years of age; universal
National Anthem: "Hymn of the Russian Federation," music by Alexander
Alexandrov and lyrics by Sergey Mikhalkov

Russia—our holy country,
Russia—our beloved country.
A mighty will, a great glory
Are your inheritance for all times!

Be glorious, our free Fatherland!
Eternal union of fraternal peoples,
Common wisdom given by our forebears,
Be glorious, our country!
We are proud of you!

From the southern seas
to the polar region
spread our forests and fields.
You are unique in the world, inimitable,
Native land protected by God!

Wide spaces for dreams and for living
Are opened for us by the coming years.
Faithfulness to our country
gives us strength
Thus it was, so it is and always will be!

CULTURAL FACT SHEET

Official Languages: Russian, Turkic languages, many others

Major Religions: Russian Orthodoxy, Islam, Judaism, Buddhism, others

Population: 144.5 million

Population Growth Rate: -0.3%

Population Density: 22 people per square mile (8 per sq km)

Population of Major Cities: Moscow: 13.2 million; St. Petersburg: 5.1 million; Volgograd: 2.7 million; Novosibirsk: 1.5 million; Yekaterinburg: 1.3 million; Smolensk: 1.2 million

Composition: 73% urban; 27% rural

Ethnic Groups: Russian 81.5%, Tatar 4%, Ukrainian 3%, Chuvash 1%, Bashkir 1%, Belarusian 0.8%, Moldavian 0.7%, other 8% (includes Chechen, German, Udmurt, Mari, Kazakh, Avar, and Armenian)

Life Expectancy: 62.5 years male, 73 years female

Time: Moscow time is Greenwich Mean Time +3 hours

Literacy Rate: 99.6% (99.7% male, 99.5% female)

National Animal: Russian brown bear (unofficial)

Famous Landmarks: Moscow: St. Basil's Cathedral, the Kremlin, Red Square; St. Petersburg: The Hermitage Museum, *The Bronze Horseman* sculpture, Peter and Paul Fortress; Volgograd: *Mother Russia* sculpture

Telephones: 30 million main lines; 19 million cellular

Internet Service Providers: 300, supplying 18 million Internet users

Current Environmental Issues: Air pollution from heavy industry, emissions of coal-fired electric plants, and transportation in major cities; industrial, municipal, and agricultural pollution of inland waterways and sea coasts; deforestation; soil erosion; soil contamination from improper application of agricultural chemicals; scattered areas of sometimes intense radioactive contamination; ground water contamination from toxic waste

National Holidays and Festivals

January 1: **New Year's Day**
January 7: **Russian Orthodox Christmas**
March/April: **Russian Orthodox Easter**
March 8: **International Women's Day**

May 1: **May Day/Labor Day**
May 9: **Victory Day**
June 12: **Independence Day**
November 7: **October Revolution Day**

GLOSSARY

atheist (AY-thee-ist) A person who does not believe in God.

babushka (beh-BOOSH-ka) A Russian grandmother; also, a kerchief traditionally worn by a Russian grandmother.

Bolshevik (BOL-shee-vik) A member of the Communist Party in Russia around the time of the 1917 Russian Revolution.

Communism (KAHM-yoo-ni-zum) A system of government in which the government owns and controls all land and property.

cosmonaut (KAHZ-meh-not) A Russian astronaut.

czar (ZAR) The title of the ruler of Russia prior to the 1917 Russian Revolution; also spelled tsar.

dacha (DAH-keh) A Russian country cottage typically used during the summer.

defect (di-FEKT) To leave one country for another, usually because of political differences.

exiled (EX-eyld) To be forced to leave one's country.

free-market economy (FREE-mar-ket ee-KAH-nuh-mee) An economic system in which businesses set their own prices for goods and services.

fresco (FRES-koh) A type of wall painting on wet plaster.

glasnost (GLAZ-nost) A Soviet policy allowing public discussion of social and political issues and freedom of expression; "openness."

icon (EYE-kon) A sacred painting in the Russian Orthodox Church.

iconostasis (ee-kah-no-STAY-sis) An altar screen that separates the sanctuary from the rest of the church.

Islam (ISS-lahm) The religious faith of Muslims.

matryoshka (ma-TRY-osh-kah) A set of wooden dolls that range in size from large to small, with each doll fitting inside another doll in the set.

Muslim (MUZ-lim) One who believes in Islam.

patriarch (PAY-tree-ark) The head priest of the Russian Orthodox Church.

perestroika (pehr-eh-STROY-kuh) A Soviet policy of economic and governmental reform established by Mikhail Gorbachev.

permafrost (PUR-meh-frost) Soil that remains permanently frozen all year.

propaganda (prah-peh-GAN-duh) False information spread for the purpose of furthering a political cause or discrediting an opposing cause.

samovar (SAH-meh-var) A large urn used to boil water for tea.

serf (SERF) A peasant who lived and worked on land owned by a wealthy lord and who was required to work for the lord as payment for rent.

steppe (STEP) A flat prairie with no trees.

taiga (TY-guh) A type of forest filled with evergreen trees.

tundra (TUHN-drah) A flat, treeless plain, much of which consists of permanently frozen soil.

FOR MORE INFORMATION

Embassy of the Russian Federation
2650 Wisconsin Avenue NW
Washington, DC 20007
(202) 298-5700
Web site: http://www.
    russianembassy.org

Russian Studies Department
Bucknell University
Lewisburg, PA 17837
Web site: http://www.departments.
    bucknell.edu/russian

The State Hermitage Museum
34 Dvortsovaya Naberezhnaya, 190000
St. Petersburg, Russia
Web site: http://www.hermitagemuseum.
    org/html_En/index.html

Web Sites

Due to the changing nature of Internet links, the Rosen Publishing Group, Inc., has developed an online list of Web sites related to the subject of this book. This site is updated regularly. Please use this link to access the list:

http://www.rosenlinks.com/pswc/russ

FOR FURTHER READING

Brewster, Hugh. *Anastasia's Album*. New York: Hyperion Books, 1996.

Costain, Meredith, and Paul Collins. *Welcome to Russia* (Countries of the World). Broomall, PA: Chelsea House Publishers, 2002.

Lychack, William. *Russia* (Games People Play!). New York: Children's Press, 1996.

Nickles, Greg. *Russia—the Culture*. New York: Crabtree Publishing, 2000.

Nickles, Greg. *Russia—the Land*. New York: Crabtree Publishing, 2000.

Nickles, Greg. *Russia—the People*. New York: Crabtree Publishing, 2000.

Plotkin, Gregory, and Rita Plotkin. *Cooking the Russian Way*. Minneapolis, MN: Lerner Publications Company, 2003.

Popescu, Julian. *Russia*. Philadelphia: Chelsea House Publishers, 1999.

Ransome, Arthur. *Favorite Russian Fairy Tales*. New York: Dover Publications, 1995.

Riordan, James. *Russian Folk-Tales*. New York: Oxford University Press, 2000.

Rogers, Stillman D. *Russia* (Enchantment of the World). New York: Children's Press, 2002.

Russia (Fiesta!). Danbury, CT: Grolier Educational, 1997.

Schomp, Virginia. *Russia: New Freedoms, New Challenges* (Exploring Cultures of the World). New York: Benchmark Books, 1996.

Welton, Jude. *Marc Chagall* (Artists in Their Time). New York: Franklin Watts, 2003.

World Book. *Christmas in Russia*. Chicago: World Book, Inc., 1997.

BIBLIOGRAPHY

CIA: The World Factbook. "Russia." Retrieved September 10, 2003 (http://www.cia.gov/cia/publications/factbook/geos/rs.html).

Dando, William A., Anna R. Carson, and Carol Z. Dando. *Russia (Modern World Nations)*. Broomall, PA: Chelsea House Publishers, 2003.

Encyclopaedia Britannica. "Russia." Retrieved August 29, 2003 (http://www.britannica.com).

Lychack, William. *Russia (Games People Play!)*. New York: Children's Press, 1996.

Nickles, Greg. *Russia—the Culture*. New York: Crabtree Publishing, 2000.

Nickles, Greg. *Russia—the People*. New York: Crabtree Publishing, 2000.

PBS.org. "Fabergé Eggs: Mementos of a Doomed Dynasty." Retrieved September 2, 2003 (http://www.pbs.org/treasuresoftheworld/a_nav/faberge_nav/main_fabfrm.html).

Plotkin, Gregory, and Rita Plotkin. *Cooking the Russian Way*. Minneapolis, MN: Lerner Publications Company, 2003.

Raleigh, Donald J. "Russia." World Book Online. Retrieved September 4, 2003 (http://www.worldbookonline.com).

Rogers, Stillman D. *Russia (Enchantment of the World)*. New York: Children's Press, 2002.

Schomp, Virginia. *Russia: New Freedoms, New Challenges* (Exploring Cultures of the World). New York: Benchmark Books, 1996.

Schulman, Colette. "Lands and Peoples: Russia." Grolier Online. Retrieved August 29, 2003 (http://www.grolieronline.com).

Warner, Elizabeth. *Russian Myths*. Austin, TX: University of Texas Press, 2002.

World Book Online. "Eastern Orthodox Churches." Retrieved September 4, 2003 (http://www.worldbookonline.com).

PRIMARY SOURCE IMAGE LIST

Page 6: St. Basil's Cathedral is located in Moscow's Red Square. It was constructed from 1551 to 1561.

Page 19: Fourth-century BC Scythian gold pectoral (necklace). Housed in the Hermitage Museum in St. Petersburg.

Page 20 (top): This seventh to sixth century BC Scythian gold stag was originally a shield decoration. This piece is housed in the Hermitage Museum in St. Petersburg.

Page 20 (bottom): *The Siege of Kozelsk* (1238), from a series of sixteenth-century chronicles written during the reign of Ivan the Terrible.

Page 22: An 1897 portrait of Ivan the Terrible by Victor Mikhailovich Vasnetsov. Housed in the Tretyakov Gallery in Moscow.

Page 23 (top): Anonymous eighteenth-century oil-on-canvas portrait of Catherine the Great. Housed in the Portraitgalerie of Schloss Ambras in Innsbruck, Austria.

Page 24: A 1905 photograph taken during the Bloody Sunday massacre outside the Winter Palace in St. Petersburg.

Page 27: A 1935 photograph of Joseph Stalin addressing the Russian public.

Page 28: This 1925 poster commemorates the Bolshevik Revolution.

Page 29: Photograph of Red Army tank maneuvers taken at a base camp near Moscow on October 24, 1935.

Page 30 (top): A 1954 photograph by Henri-Cartier Bresson showing women and children in line at a grocery store in St. Petersburg.

Page 30 (bottom): A 1988 photograph by Bruno Barbey showing a crowd of Russians examining posters calling for glasnost.

Page 32: Photograph of Boris Yeltsin taken by Michael Samoieden on August 20, 1991, at the Russian Parliament in Moscow.

Page 34: Eleventh-century tablet written in Cyrillic, discovered in Novgorod in July 2000.

Page 37 (top): An 1862 panel of Saint Cyril (826–869) and Saint Methodius (c. 815–885) by the Bulgarian School. Housed in the Museum of History of Sofia, Sofia, Bulgaria.

Page 38: The last front page of *Pravda* newspaper, dated March 13, 1991.

Page 40: A 1901 color lithograph by Ivan Jakovlevitch Bilibin. Housed in the Kunst and Geschichte Archive, Berlin, Germany.

Page 41: An illustration of Baba the Witch from *Old Peter's Russian Tales* by D. Mitrokhin, 1915.

Page 42: *The Very Beautiful Vassilissa*, painted by Ivan Bilibin in 1899. Housed at the Bibliothéque des Arts Decoratifs in Paris, France.

Page 44: A 1901 color lithograph by Ivan Bilibin depicting the story of the Firebird. Housed at the Kunst and Geschichte Archive Collection, Berlin, Germany.

Page 45: *The Snow Maiden* by Victor Mikhailovitch Vasnetsov. Housed in the Tretyakov Gallery, Moscow.

Page 46: An undated photograph of Czar Nicholas II and his family.

Page 54: A 1957 photograph of a parade in Red Square commemorating the fortieth anniversary of the Bolshevik Revolution, taken by Elliot Erwitt.

Page 58: Fifteenth-century painting of the archangel Michael by Andrei Rublev.

Page 59: The Grand Monastery of Zagorsk, built during the fourteenth century.

Page 61: Assumption Cathedral in Moscow, built between 1475 and 1479 by architect Aristotele Fioravanti.

Page 64: Two twelfth- to thirteenth-century Seljuk style pages of the Koran. Housed in the Museum of the Holy Ma'sumeh Shrine in Qom, Iran.

Page 68: *The Street in the Village* painted by Marc Chagall (1887–1985) in 1976. From a private collection.

Page 69: Russian icon painted on wood, entitled *Mother of God*, circa seventeenth century. Housed in the Tretjakov Gallery in Moscow, Russia.

Page 70 (top): *Transverse Line* by Wassily Kandinsky, 1923. Housed in the Kunstsammlung Nordrhein-Westfalen in Düsseldorf, Germany.

Page 70 (bottom): Circa 1960s photograph of artist Marc Chagall in his house, called La Coline, in St.-Paul-de-Vence, France.

Page 71: A 1967 photograph of *Mother Russia*, a monument erected on Mamayev Hill in Volgograd (formerly Stalingrad). Sculptor Yevgeny Vuchetich constructed the monument from 1963 to 1967.

Page 72 (top): Alexander Rodchenko made the collage *The Construction of the USSR* around 1920. Today this work is located in the Museum of the Revolution in Moscow, Russia.

Page 73: Carl Fabergé designed this Easter egg, which contains a model of the cruiser *Memory of Azov*, in 1891. The goldsmith Michael Perchin supervised the translucent enameling of this egg. Housed in the Armory of the Kremlin, Moscow, Russia.

Page 78: Pytor Ilich Tchaikovsky's notes in pencil for his opera *The Queen of Spades*. Presented to the Tchaikovsky Museum in Klin, Russia, in 1928 on the thirty-fifth anniversary of Tchaikovsky's death.

Page 79: An 1827 portrait of poet Aleksandr Pushkin by Wassilj A. Tropinin. Housed in the Pushkin Museum, Moscow, Russia.

Page 81 (top): Undated photograph of writer Anton Chekov (1860–1904).

Page 81 (bottom): Original playbill from a 1980's production of *Uncle Vanya*, performed at the Vaudeville Theater in the Strand, London.

Page 82 (top): Circa 1900 photograph of writer Maksim Gorky. Housed at the Archiv für Kunst und Geschichte, Berlin, Germany.

Page 82 (bottom): Hand-written draft of Fyodor Dostoevsky's 1880 speech on Pushkin. Includes author's margin notes.

Page 83: Photograph of writer Leo Tolstoy in his birthplace, the Russian village of Yasnaya Polyana, by Yevgeny Kassin. This photograph, an early example of color photography, was taken on May 23, 1908.

Page 84: Undated, signed photograph of composer Pytor Ilich Tchaikovsky.

Page 104: A 1920 poster celebrating the Bolshevik Revolution, created for the Nikolai M. Kochergin studio. From a private collection.

INDEX

About the Author

Suzanne J. Murdico is a freelance writer who has authored more than twenty books for children and teens. She lives near Tampa with her husband, Vinnie, and their cats, Max and Boo.

Designer: Geri Fletcher; **Cover Designer:** Tahara Anderson;
Editor: Mark Beyer; **Photo Researcher:** Fernanda Rocha